Divine
APPOINTMENTS

More Soulwinning Stories
by Walter L. Wilson

Christ Walk Publications is a division of On To Victory
Press, a ministry of Falls Baptist Church, N69W12703
Appleton Avenue, Menomonee Falls, WI 53051.

Christ Walk Publications is committed to providing
biblical resources to equip God's people, both
individually and corporately, to walk with Him and to
teach others to do the same.

All Scripture quotations are taken from the Holy Bible,
King James Version.

Cover design and Layout by Joe Mueller
Edited by Yvonne Sheppard
Special thanks to our proofreaders

Editor's Note: The original spellings and capitalizations
of the author have been retained in this edition and
reflect the style of his day.

Originally published as *The Romance of a Doctor's Visits* by
Bible Institute Colportage Association. First edition
(January 1, 1935). The original work is public domain,
however the edit and design work is copyrighted by
Christ Walk Publications.

ISBN: 978-1-951455-12-5
Printed in the United States of America

Contents

.

Publisher's Note

This volume was originally published by Dr. Wilson under the title of *The Romance of a Doctor's Visits.* We are pleased to publish this volume again under a new name for this generation. A few of the stories found in the original volume have not been included in this edition as they are included in *Just What the Doctor Ordered*, also available from Christ Walk Publications.

A Little Lad Stopped Praying

At the close of an evening service in which I had endeavored to make known God's way of salvation, clearly and plainly, I went to the door of the church to greet the friends as they passed out. Standing by the door was a gentleman holding a lad of about twelve years of age by the hand. It was his son and he was in tears.

The father approached me, saying, "Doctor, Jimmie would like to be saved. Will you talk with him?"

I knew the little lad well, and knew that he had been raised in a home where the Bible was read and where prayer was offered to God daily. I said to the little fellow: "Would you like the Lord Jesus to save you tonight?"

"Yes, I would," he replied, "but I do not know how to come to Jesus; I cannot find Him."

Taking his hand, I led him to the front of the church in order to escape the noise of the friends who were visiting around the door. Up in the choir-loft we could be alone. There I said to him, "Jimmie, will you kneel with me and thank the Lord for everything that you can thank Him for?"

"Yes," he said, "I will do that."

"Very well, Jimmie, if you will do that, I will tell you some additional things to be thankful for."

We then knelt together to pray. I prayed first and thanked the Savior for His wonderful work at Calvary, and for His

Word of truth. I asked the Holy Spirit to reveal the Lord Jesus to the heart of this dear boy, and to open his understanding so that he would know the value and the virtue of the precious blood of Christ.

When I had ceased, little Jimmie prayed, saying, "Lord Jesus, I thank Thee for coming to this earth to save me. I thank Thee for dying on the cross for my sins. I thank Thee for coming to be my Savior."

There was a silence after this. I was kneeling with my eyes closed, and waited quite a while for Jimmie to continue, but he did not. When the silence became embarrassing, I looked around to see what Jimmie was doing, and found he was kneeling upright on his knees and smiling at me. "Why did you stop praying?" I asked.

"Because," he said, "I just found out that Jesus really did it."

The joy of the Lord filled his face, the tears had stopped, and his smile told of the inward peace.

While he was thanking the Savior, the Spirit revealed the truth of the statements he had heard from the Scriptures. He had known what the Bible said about Christ and His work at the cross, but he had not believed that it was for himself. He had not personally applied it to his own soul. He had not realized that the Lord Jesus came to save him, as though there was no one else to save.

Jimmie was a new boy. He hurried back to his father with a buoyant step and a radiant spirit to tell him that Jesus really did it. He is now a grown lad, carrying his Bible and seeking to live a life pleasing to the One who bought him with His precious blood.

How often people make the mistake of believing the facts without applying them to their own hearts! To acknowledge the truth of the Gospel is not sufficient; it must be applied to the soul and accepted personally in order to have value. The fact that Christ is a wonderful Savior is a blessed truth. Each one, however, must come to Him personally and accept Him as his own personal Lord and Savior (John 1:12). To believe that a doctor is able to prescribe the proper remedy is only to acknowledge the truth of the facts. To engage that doctor to handle your own case, and to take charge of you and your disease, brings the application of the facts to your own life. Do not miss Heaven by missing the Savior!

How often we find in Christian homes a belief of the facts and an orthodox faith in the Bible without a personal washing in the blood of the Lamb. These are absolutely essential.

Do you have a radiant step and a radiant spirit?

The Nurse Found Her Debt Was Paid

A Christian nurse in a certain great hospital was as interested in the souls of those about her as she was in the bodies of her patients. She was particularly interested in the other nurses with whom she constantly associated. The duties of the nurses and the hours during which they must serve kept many of them from attending religious services, and therefore it was no uncommon thing for them to drift away from the faith which they had learned at home.

Upon one occasion, this saved nurse brought with her to the church another nurse who had expressed a desire to hear the Gospel preached by a physician. I saw the two girls in the service and knew that one of them was a stranger. At the close of the meeting, my friend brought the new nurse forward and introduced her. Thinking immediately of her salvation, I asked, "Are you a saved nurse, or are you a lost nurse?"

"Oh," she replied, "I am a Christian; I joined the church twelve years ago."

"It is certainly a pleasure to know that you are interested in these matters; but do you know that there are two kinds of church members?"

"No," she said, "what are they?"

"Saved ones and lost ones," I answered; "I wonder which kind you are!"

This reply seemed to be a little disconcerting to the nurse, and she did not answer at once. I could see the Christian nurse off at one side, quietly praying that the Lord would do a good work in the heart of her friend. How blessed it is that we may help the soul winner by prayer and so have a part in the harvest!

After a few thoughtful moments, the nurse looked up and said, "Really, doctor, I do not know whether I am saved or lost. I came to this service to find out. I am not at all clear in my mind about the way of salvation and feel that I should know."

"Did you ever sing that beautiful hymn, 'Jesus Paid It All'?"

"Oh, yes," she said, "that is in almost every hymn book that I have seen. It is an old song, and I like it very much."

"Well, tell me, nurse, did Jesus pay it all for you, or did He not?" Again, the nurse bowed her head in meditation. She was a thoughtful girl and was not to be hurried into any statement that she did not understand. Finally, she said, as she looked up, "I wish I knew whether He did pay it all. I do not feel that He has."

I answered at once, "Would you prefer to go by your feelings in the matter, or would you be willing to believe what the Word of God says about it?"

"I do not want to be fooled," she answered, "I want to know the truth. What does the Bible say about it?"

"It is finished," I replied. "Jesus said this on the cross as He was dying for you, and it is recorded in John 19:30. If He said, 'It is finished,' surely it must be finished, do you not think so? Again, let me ask you, nurse, did Jesus finish the work of salvation for you, and did He pay all of your debt?"

We had been standing by the pulpit, but when she heard these words and this question, she turned from me, stepped over a little to the front row of seats and knelt down with her head and arms upon the seat. I slipped over quickly and knelt beside her to hear what she was saying to the Lord, and these were her words: "Lord Jesus, I never knew before that You had paid my debt on the cross. I knew you had died for sinners, but I did not know that it was for me. You did pay my debt, and you said, 'It is finished'; I thank you for it, Lord Jesus. I believe my debt is paid, and oh, what a peace you have given to my heart."

The saved nurse also had knelt on the other side of her friend, and as this simple prayer of faith was ended, we both said, "Amen," and thanked God for another work of grace in a hungry heart.

It was not convenient for me to visit that particular hospital again for a number of days, perhaps a week. When I did go, I sought to find the newly saved nurse and to see whether she had truly trusted Christ, and if she had His peace and joy in her heart. I found that she was working on one of the upper floors and was in the diet kitchen. Approaching the kitchen, I looked through the serving window and saw my friend in the far corner of the room making up some fresh trays. Calling to her, I said, "Nurse, tell me, did Jesus pay it all, or did He fail in the attempt?"

She stopped her work, hurried quickly to the window, and with her face wreathed in smiles, and with happiness in her heart, said, "Doctor, Jesus did pay it all; He paid it all for me. If you had told me two weeks ago that it was possible for a person to have Heaven on earth as I have had it this week, I would have laughed at you and thought it was preposterous. Now I have Heaven in my heart, for I belong to the Lord Jesus Christ."

You, too, may enjoy Heaven on earth if you will only learn to know and love the Savior who "Paid it all."

A Dead Undertaker Came to Life

In the beautiful little city of C——, there was a home filled with sorrow. The mother had been called away by the Lord, leaving a grief-torn family and many sorrowing friends who loved her dearly.

Through the radio in this home, the Lord had spoken to their hearts, and in the hour of their distress they requested me to come and conduct the funeral service — the invitation coming through a relative who was a close friend of mine.

A cold rain was falling on the day of the funeral, and the road to the cemetery was not paved. Because of the deep mud on the road, I decided to leave my car in the town; and so I asked permission of the undertaker to ride with him in the hearse to the cemetery. This request he readily granted. As we drove along slowly through the mire, I said to him — he was a young man of about thirty, "What do you suppose the Bible means by saying, 'Let the dead bury their dead'?" (Matthew 8:22).

"There isn't any Scripture like that in the Bible," he very promptly replied. "Yes, there is," I assured him.

"Well," he answered, "it must be a wrong translation, because it doesn't make any sense. How could a dead person bury a dead person?"

"No, it is not a wrong translation," I said. "These words were spoken by the Lord Jesus Himself. He always spoke words of truth, and did not play with the feelings nor the imaginations of His hearers."

The young undertaker flipped the cigarette he was smoking out of the window, and said, "Do you know anything about me, doctor? Has anyone told you about my life?"

"No," I replied, "Why do you ask?"

"Because I have been burying many people lately, and it has caused me to think about my own case. Last night after supper, I got out the Bible and read until two o'clock this morning, trying to find out how to become a Christian."

"Did you find out how to be one?" I inquired."No," he said, "when I finished I was just as much in the dark as before; but tell me, what did Jesus mean by those words?"

The peculiar passage was so suited to this man's mind, that it was an easy matter now to tell him about the Savior. I said to him: "You are a dead undertaker in the front of this hearse, driving out to the cemetery to bury the dead friend in the back of the hearse. That friend is dead to her family, and you are dead to God. She does not respond to their caresses, their calls, their commands; neither do you respond to the call and love of God."

"You are right about that," he said; "I cannot find God; I cannot talk to Him, for I do not know where He is, nor how to reach Him. Christ is right; I certainly need some kind of a change in my life to make me a real Christian."

The auto was moving slowly, for the road was difficult, and we had plenty of time for conversation. Opening my Bible, I read to him John 10:10—"I am come that they might have life, and that they might have it more abundantly." Explaining the verse, I asserted that Christ Jesus had come to give the dead sinner—dead in his trespasses and sins—the gift of eternal life. This life is the life that is in the heart of the Lord Himself. It is a new nature imparted to the soul, so that the person naturally lives a Godly life and loves the One who gave him the life.

"May I obtain that life?" he said, "and when may I have it?"

"Just now, right here in this hearse you may accept Jesus Christ"; and I assured him that by trusting this Savior, believing in His precious blood shed for Him at Calvary, he, too, would receive everlasting life immediately. "Here is the Scripture; let me read it to you slowly, as you drive the car. 'He that hath the Son hath life; and he that hath not the Son of God hath not life' (I John 5:12). This Savior is on the throne waiting to give you this life the moment you believe in Him and trust the work that He did for you at Calvary when He died for your sins."

"I'll take Him," he said; "I never did know what the Savior did when He died, nor why He did it. It never entered my mind that it was for me. Of course it must have been for me, for I know there is no other Savior and no one that even claims to be. He must have suffered for my sins and I believe it.

We arrived at the cemetery with a live undertaker, though we had started on the journey with a dead one. He who was "dead in trespasses and sins" (Ephesians 2:1) was now alive in Christ, having trusted Him who gave His life for his salvation. We returned to the city after the burial, and along the slow journey home I had the privilege of telling him further of God's imputed righteousness, the divine gift of pardon, and the blessed forgiveness in grace which is made possible by the shed blood of the Savior.

Examine your own heart, my friend, and see whether you, too, are "dead" in trespasses and in sins. Christ will give you "life" if you come to Him by faith and trust in Him for your soul's salvation.

The Worst Sin in the Best Stenographer

Three physicians occupied a suite of rooms in a great office building devoted to the medical profession. These men had engaged a number of young ladies for secretarial work at different times. None had given such satisfactory service as a Miss B——, who seemed especially fitted for this type of work. She was pleasant in her manner and quite efficient in all of her service.

One evening about half-past four, this lady, who was a stranger to me, telephoned my office and requested an interview at five o'clock, which was granted. She was soon at the door in a taxicab, and came into the office. I could see that she was greatly agitated about something, and since I did not know that she was in a doctor's office, asked her whether she wanted to see me as a physician or as a minister. "As a minister," she said, "for I work in a doctor's office."

I asked her to tell me the condition of her soul, and what her particular trouble might be.

"I am a terrible sinner," she replied; "no one knows it but God and me. It is making me most wretched — in fact, so much so, that I fear my mind will give way under the strain. It is such a horrible sin that I cannot even tell you what it is. I know that God will never forgive me for it, and I am not seeking that; I know there is no remedy. I only want you to tell me whether there is any way that I can endure this agony any longer."

Such a case as this had never before come to my attention. I asked her to kneel with me while we prayed together for wisdom and light. After praying, the Holy Spirit put it into my heart to find for her those Scriptures which assure us that all sins may be washed away by the blood of Christ. I found a number of such passages, but before giving them to her, I pleaded for more information concerning her case. She steadfastly refused, but assured me that no other human being was involved in the sin; that she had sinned only against the Lord Jesus and no one else.

We then turned to the Scriptures, such as "And you, being dead in your sins and the uncircumcision of your flesh, hath he quickened together with him, having forgiven you all trespasses; Blotting out the handwriting of ordinances that was against us, which was contrary to us, and took it out of the way, nailing it to his cross" (Colossians 2:13-14); and "But he was wounded for our transgressions, he was bruised for our iniquities: the chastisement of our peace was upon him; and with his stripes we are healed. All we like sheep have gone astray; we have turned every one to his own way; and the Lord hath laid on him the iniquity of us all" (Isaiah 53:5-6). None of these gave her any help or relief.

Again, I urged her to tell me the character of the sin. I assured her, that as a doctor, I could not help my patients until I knew the symptoms and found the seat of the disease. The fireman would not be content with throwing water on smoke; he must find the fire before he could put it out. Thus I encouraged her, for it was quite evident that her sin was not such a one as was common among men, but must be of some peculiar character which would need special Scripture passages to solve.

Supper time had now arrived and the gong summoned us to the table. I requested that supper be reserved for a while, because the situation was too acute to leave just at this juncture. The contact was too vital. Continuing with her, I said: "I really think we should not continue any longer unless you are willing to tell me your need, in order that I may bring to you God's Word which will meet that need."

She then laid aside her reserve and told a most remarkable story of her attitude towards the person of Christ. It was the most unusual and peculiar attitude I have ever heard from any human lips. It was unbelievable in its character, were it not that it came from the lips of one having that experience.

"This is none other than a demon, Miss B——. No other power on earth would put such thoughts in your mind. The devil hates Christ and would like to keep you from trusting Him; therefore he has given you this strange attitude. The Lord Jesus is the only one who can conquer Satan. He will give you the victory just now, if you will trust Him."

We turned and read Acts 13:38-39, where the Holy Spirit has recorded: "Be it known unto you therefore, men and brethren, that through this man is preached unto you the forgiveness of sins: and by him all that believe are justified from all things, from which ye could not be justified by the law of Moses." Her attention was called to the two uses of the word "all" in this verse. The first "all" included herself, the second "all" included her sins. We read the verse over several times, while I pressed upon her these two words.

It was seven o'clock before her heart yielded and her mind accepted the statement of God's Word concerning that word "all." Finally she yielded.

"It doesn't seem right to me," she said, "but since God has said it, I must believe that it is so. What wonderful grace on His part that He should make such a provision for one so utterly wicked."

"Will you tell the Lord Jesus that you believe Him?" I inquired. "If you will trust Him just now, you should tell Him so; then He will give you His peace and the assurance that all your sins are blotted out." She readily agreed, and as we knelt together beside the wicker chair, she poured out her heart in gratitude to the One who would blot out such terrible sins.

Bring Him your sins, my friends, whatever they are and however so many they may be, and Christ will pardon and cleanse you from all sin.

How Many Sins Are against You?

It was the custom in our office for the new stenographers to be broken in for the new work in my department. On a certain day, the office manager introduced a young lady who had applied for a position. Some mail had accumulated ready for handling, so I asked her to be seated, while I gave her the first letters in her new position.

Just before dictating, I said to her, "Miss M——, are you a good girl or a bad girl?"

She looked at me with astonishment, her face flushed a bit, as she replied: "Why, I am a good girl. Has someone been telling you otherwise about me?" It was quite evident that the thought of being bad was rather abhorrent to her.

"How good are you?" I asked. "Are you real good, or just a little bit good?"

"I want you to know that there is nothing wrong about me," she replied, "and I cannot understand why you should ask such a question."

"How old are you, Miss M——?" was my next inquiry.

"Really, sir," she said, "I cannot see what that has to do with taking your dictation."

She certainly was ruffled and disturbed by these questions which to her mind were quite apart from the job for which she was engaged. I looked at her rather intently, and then, taking a pencil and paper, I said, "I would think that you were about thirty years of age, is that right?"

"You can say anything you please," she said, "I came to take your letters."

"Very well," I continued, "if you are about thirty, then you have had at least twenty years of personal accountability. You may not have been responsible for the first ten years, but you are for the last twenty."

I wrote down the twenty on my pad, and said: "During each of these twenty years you have lived 365 days. Let us multiply these together. You will notice that you have lived 7,300 days for which you are responsible, and perhaps you have committed one sin on each of these days. Do you think you have done so?" I inquired.

"I am quite sure that I have," she said, looking rather puzzled at the figures on the pad.

"If you have 7,300 sins against you today, Miss M——, would you call that being a good girl or a bad girl?"

"I certainly wouldn't think that I was very good," she said, "but I never had figured it up before. It may be I am not as good as I thought I was. Really, I think that I have committed many more than one sin a day."

"Perhaps you have," I answered. "There are sins of omission, sins of commission, sins of ignorance, and sins of presumption. Do you think you might have committed one of each of these each day?"

"Yes, and more than that," was her quick response.

By this time my friend was getting quite interested. Her mind was running back over her life, and no doubt her memory was filled with things which she would like to have forgotten.

"Shall we make it ten a day?" I asked, kindly. "Yes, that is not too many," she answered.

The pad lay conveniently near, where she could continually see the figures, I multiplied the 7,300 by ten, and wrote in large figures 73,000 and underneath it the words: "Sins committed by a good girl."

Turning to her again and watching her countenance closely, I said, "In view of these figures, Miss M——, do you still think you are a good girl, or are you a bad girl?" Her face was flushed, and the agitation of her mind and heart were evident. She was deeply interested now.

"Do you think, Miss M——, that there might have been some days when there were than ten sins?"

"Doctor," she replied, "if you only knew what a temper I have and how easy it is for me to do some things that are wrong, you would not need to ask me that question. I know I have been unusually sinful on some occasions. Really, I never dreamed how sinful I am."

This was the confession which I knew preceded salvation. It was easy now to turn to the gospel story and tell of the Savior and His power to save.

"Christ Jesus came into the world to save sinners," I quoted, (I Timothy 1:15). "He knew that you would be a sinner, and would need Him. He knew that you could not change yourself, nor save your own soul. He knew that you could not blot out the black record of these many sins by any efforts of your own. That is the reason He came to save you. Would you like to have that Savior blot out all of these sins today?"

"I am not sure," she answered. "This is all so new to me."

Seeing her perplexity and astonishment, I said, "We will talk about this again when you wish it," and took up the letters to give the dictation.

The next morning, when I came to the office, Miss M—— had preceded me and was sitting at my desk, waiting for a continuation of the conference.

"I could not sleep last night," she said. "My sins kept coming before me like a great mountain. I realized, as I had never done before, how very wicked I am. Is there no remedy for me? No way of blotting out these sins?"

We turned at once to the precious Word of God which is so full of the remedy, and which gives such a clear answer to this question. Our first passage was Isaiah 44:22 — "I have blotted out, as a thick cloud, thy transgressions, and, as a cloud, thy sins: return unto me; for I have redeemed thee."

"The One against whom you have sinned, Miss M——, is the One who has found a way to blot out those sins. That way is by Calvary. It is the blood of Christ that blots out sins, and God has ordained it so Himself: 'But if we walk in the light, as he is in the light, we have fellowship one with another, and the blood of Jesus Christ his Son cleanseth us from all sin. If we say that we have no sin, we deceive ourselves, and the truth is not in us. If we confess our sins, he is faithful and just to forgive us our sins, and to cleanse us from all unrighteousness' (I John 1:7-9). It was God's way to send the Lord Jesus to die for you. 'The Lord hath laid on him the iniquity of us all' (Isaiah 53:6). Peter also recorded that He bore our sins in his own body on the tree (I Peter 2:24). Christ will take those sins away from you, if you but trust Him today with your soul. Listen now to these words by Paul: 'In whom we have redemption through his blood, the forgiveness of sins, according to the riches of his grace' (Ephesians 1:7).

"You have the privilege, Miss M——, of coming to Christ Jesus just as you are in your sins, accepting Him as your Savior, and letting Him accept you. He cleanses those who bring their defilement to Him. That is His work. 'As many as received him, to them gave he power to become the sons of God, even to them that believe on his name' (John 1:12). Will you receive Him just now?"

The tears and the trembling hands indicated the deep work that God was doing in that heart. The Holy Spirit had convicted her of sin, and now He would reveal to her the Lord Jesus Christ, the Savior of sinners.

"I will accept Him," she answered, slowly and deliberately. "I want to be saved, and I want to be saved right now. I cannot go on in my sins any longer."

"Then tell Him," I urged; "tell Him now that you accept Him, that you trust in His precious blood, and thank Him for bearing away your sins on Calvary."

With bowed head, she did so, and rested her all on the Lord Jesus Christ. Her subsequent life in the office, and later in a neighboring city, has testified to the good work of God by which she was born again.

You, too, my friend, should examine yourself to see just how bad you are. Then when the terrible facts are revealed to your heart, you will quickly flee to Jesus Christ, who is the Refuge from the storm of wrath.

Soulwinning at Sixty Miles an Hour

A Bible conference was being held in the little city of S——
recently. It was to convene for two days, with three meetings a
day, and each service was to be held in a different church. The
Lord very graciously reached the hearts of many. Some of the
lost souls were saved, some backsliders came home to the
Father's house, and the Christians were edified.

Just before the closing service on Saturday night, the pastor
who was entertaining me, and who had promised to drive me
to a neighboring town twenty miles distant to catch the train,
informed me that a young man had requested the pleasure of
taking me to that city after the service. He further mentioned
that this friend was the son of one of the pastors of the city. He
had been attending college, and was home only for the week-
end. To this I agreed, hoping that the student had a desire to
know the Lord better, and was choosing this method of having
a personal visit with me about the matter.

The meeting closed that evening at half-past eight, and in
five minutes I was able to get away from the many friends and
hurry out to the waiting car. The auto was of a very ancient
vintage, sometimes known as a "rattling good car." It did not
look very safe, in view of the fact that we must make the drive
in twenty-five minutes. The train left at nine o'clock, and
therefore we must waste no time on the gravel road which took
us to the station in the neighboring city.

As soon as I had entered the auto and was seated, my young friend opened the conversation by saying: "I hope that you are not offended because I requested the pleasure of taking you to the train, instead of the pastor. I wanted to have a talk with you about my own condition, and did not know of any other way in which I could have a time alone with you."

We were now driving out of the little village and were on the gravel road. The speedometer kept climbing until it reached sixty miles. The darkness around us, together with the loose gravel underneath, did not make me feel altogether comfortable at that speed.

"Tell me about yourself," I ventured, between breaths.

"My name is John T——, he said, "and I am a son of the pastor with whom you had your service yesterday morning. My father thinks I am a Christian. I went through the training classes, was confirmed, have been baptized, and have sought to live a clean, good life, as my father so well prepared me for."

I was holding on to the sides of the car as we swayed along the road, but managed to reply, saying, "You might have all this, John, and simply be a lovely lost sinner with a wonderful religious experience."

"I know that," he said, "and I have realized, since going off to college, that although I had my father's faith, I have never made it my own faith. I have not been able to stand the test at school, and have fallen into ways and habits that would hurt my father terribly if he knew it. I do not want to be defeated nor deceived."

My companion was a delightful young fellow of about twenty years of age. I admired his candor and honesty as well as his earnestness in seeking for the light and truth.

"May I remind you," I said, "of a beautiful old passage of Scripture? — 'For God so loved the world, that he gave his only begotten Son, that whosoever believeth on him should not perish, but have everlasting life.' You will notice, John, that here is God's remedy for sin, and His way to avoid perishing. I know that is what you want. You neither want your soul to perish, nor your life to be lost. Christ will save you from both."

By this time the car had become quite unsteady. I suggested to him that we slow down the car, for it would be better to be late for the train than early across the "divide." To this he readily assented. When we had slowed down to about forty miles, I prayed that our Lord would hold the train as long as necessary while my friend heard the Gospel and accepted the Savior.

"Please explain to me, doctor, just how it is that Jesus saves a fellow? It is not at all clear to me. I have had lots of religious teaching, but really I know very little about how God forgives sins, and that is what I want to know." This opening was certainly the work of the Holy Spirit in his heart.

"John, this verse tells clearly that God sent His Son to save you, because you need Him. No one else can save you but Jesus. The Savior found, however, that you had many sins in your life [at this he nodded his head]; therefore it was necessary for Him to put those sins away in a righteous manner. He must take the punishment for you, suffer for your sins on the cross, and bear your sins in His own body on the tree."

The car was slowing down still more, as John sought to calm himself and to dry the tears from his eyes. "It is not enough, John, for you to know these facts. You must accept the gift that God has given, so that your own case and cause is committed to that Savior," I explained.

We were now on a straight stretch of road, so that the driving was easy. Turning to me and running very slowly, he said: "Of course, Christ cannot save me unless He has me. I will accept that gift; I will just now let Him have me and my sins. I believe that He will save me from perishing. Why did I never understand this before? How dumb I have been. I have read John 3:16 many times. Why did I never see that I must accept the gift and have Christ for my own self? Thank you so much, doctor, for showing this truth to me so plainly."

We had now arrived at the town of Y—— and the time was exactly nine o'clock. As we approached the depot, we found that a freight train was moving slowly out of the town on a track between our car and the station, where the passenger train was standing. I prayed that the Lord would hold the train until the freight had passed, so that we might reach it. Of course He did so. We hurried through the station, and the conductor held the train until I purchased my ticket, and then immediately it pulled out. I stood on the steps and waved goodbye to my friend, who called out to me, "Good-bye! He saved me; thank you."

Has He saved you?

Singing at Eighty

One afternoon, as I was busy at my desk, an old gentleman entered the office, walking with a cane, and carrying a derby hat in the other hand. It could be seen that the storms of many winters had injured his frail old body and that some heavy burden was crushing the heart.

After extending a cordial invitation to be seated, he did so. "I am glad to meet you, sir. What is your name?" I inquired.

"My name is B———," he said. "For quite some time I have been wanting to see you, because I have no joy in my life nor peace in my heart, and I am sure that the reason for this is that I am not a saved man. For many years I have been in the church. In fact, I became a member when I was about twenty years old. My life has been one of 'ups and downs' with a lot of trouble and plenty of sins."

The old gentleman was very calm, but it was quite apparent that in his heart there was a great anxiety over his condition and his future. He looked at me very closely after telling his story and seemed to wait for a reply, which I was slow to give until I should know more about his need. Because of my hesitation, he continued: "I have been listening to your morning Bible lessons on the radio for some years. I did not know what was wrong with my soul until one day you explained the need of the lost sinner for eternal life. I knew I did not have this gift and sought opportunity since then to see you and find out how to obtain this gift from God."

"Are you a lost sinner?" I inquired. "You see, the Savior came to save lost men, and my experience is that He does not come to those who have no need of Him, and who, therefore, are quite satisfied without Him. If you are a helpless sinner, needing the Savior to deliver you, I am quite sure He will do it."

"I am lost," he said, "and that is the reason I came down to have this visit. My life has been spent in disobedience and rebellion, and I know I deserve to be punished and shall be, unless God will forgive. Do you think He will?"

"Let us turn to the Scripture and see what we may find in God's own Word," I answered. My Bible was at hand, lying on the desk, and we soon found I Peter 2:24. "Please listen to this message, Mr. B——. I will read it to you slowly, for I want you to get every word of it and to understand what it says." He was a little hard of hearing, so I read loudly and clearly these words: "Who his own self bare our sins in his own body on the tree."

"Wait a moment," he interrupted. "Will you please read those words to me again?"

It is indeed a blessed sight to see the Word of God taking hold of a human heart, bringing conviction and then turning that heart to Jesus Christ. This aged friend was grasping for salvation and peace, and was only waiting until he would clearly know from the Scriptures God's wonderful remedy. I complied with his request and read the passage again. It was indeed a pleasure to witness his facial expression, as the words reached his ears. He was in a deep study, listening most attentively, and as I finished the words, again he leaned forward and said most anxiously: "Please do not be impatient with me; I am not trifling at all with this matter. Will you please be so good as to read those words to me again the third time?"

The Word of God tells the Truth of God, and does the Work of God. I repeated the passage to him, emphasizing the different words, and again intently watching his face. I could see that the truth of the portion was penetrating his heart and was being received by him gladly. His thoughtful expression revealed the fact that he was studying the statement of the Word of God, without a question or a doubt.

"The One this passage is referring to, Mr. B——, is the Lord Jesus," I explained. "He came to bear your sins away and to blot them out, because you could not pay the price, and He did not you to be lost." Mr. B—— listened to this message and then slowly arose, took his cane and derby, and started away.

"Wait a moment, Mr. B——," I cried. "Do remain a little and let me help you to see the Savior and His work for you. Please do not go away without finding Christ and having your soul saved by Him."

My friend paused a moment, removed his hat again, and said very earnestly and happily: "I do not need to wait any longer; I am going home to praise the Savior because He took all of my sins away and they are gone. The Bible says, 'He bore my sins,' and I believe He did. I can sing now; my heart is glad, for the load is gone." He replaced his hat and slowly made his way to the door, going home to sing at eighty.

Let me urge the reader of this story to settle the matter in early life. Give our Lord not only your soul to save and keep, but your life to preserve and make fruitful. He loves to redeem and He loves to enrich. Will you let Him have all of yourself just now?

What Happened When Two Judges Met

A telephone call came to the office one day, and upon answering it, a woman's voice asked: "Could you spare the time to meet my father at the L—— Hotel tomorrow? He lives out of the city and will come in on the bus line if you will give him a little of your time. He is very anxious to see you about an important matter, but being old and rather feeble, he feels that he cannot go out to your office."

This seemed to be a call from God, and I was happy to answer that it would be a pleasure to meet her father at whatever hour he might find it convenient to come. "At two o'clock in the afternoon would be the best time," she said, so this arrangement was agreed upon.

The next day I called at the hotel and found, sitting in the lobby, a very old gentleman, having a long white beard, beautiful white hair and large bushy eyebrows. I approached him and asked whether he was waiting to see someone, to which he replied that he was waiting for the doctor who had promised to meet him there at two o'clock. After introducing myself to him, we followed his suggestion and found seats on the mezzanine floor where we could be alone for our conversation.

"My name," he said, "is Judge A——. I have been a judge in the county court at M—— (a city not far from Kansas City) for many years. I am an old man as you can see, and have sent many men to the penitentiary. I am now nearing the end of my own life and I know quite well that the great Judge of all the earth will send me to His penitentiary, for I have not been a Christian nor made any provision whatever for the sins that are recorded against me. I have come to you, doctor, to see if there is any remedy for an old man whose life has been spent in worldly pursuits, with no fear of God and no Christian training."

It was interesting to observe, with mingled feelings, that here was a life spent in the service of his fellow-man, enjoying the blessings of God, but untouched by the grace of God and unmoved by His goodness. I could see that the judge was not trifling. He was in real earnest. Life at eighty is not full of foolishness. Things more serious occupy the mind and heart. The judge was facing death and after death the judgment (Hebrews 9:27).

The one who had judged others realized that now he must be judged himself. He knew that the record was filled with sins of every kind and character. He remembered that no one had been engaged to defend him at this great bar of justice. He was aware of the fact, too, that no provision had been made for the pleading of his cause; and he realized that there were no extenuating circumstances which could be presented to the Judge for the willful sins of many years. He felt that his case was hopeless.

Taking my Bible, I turned to John 5:24. Here we read those wonderful words: "Verily, verily, I say unto you, he that heareth my word and believeth on him that sent me, hath everlasting life, and shall not come into judgment; but is passed from death unto life." As those words were read slowly: "Shall not come into judgment," the judge became very attentive. His curiosity was aroused at once. "I never heard those words before," he said. "What is the meaning of the passage? Is it possible that a sinful man may escape the judgment?"

My aged friend was quite familiar with judgments, courts and trials, with all the accompanying evidence and arguments. These subjects had been his portion for many years. It was the judgment he feared and which he wanted to escape. No wonder these five great words from the lips of the Lord Jesus stirred his soul with a wonderful hope. His whole desire now was to know how this statement could be true in his case.

In order to explain the passage and answer his question, I chose Colossians 2:14, where these words are recorded: "Blotting out the handwriting of ordinances that was against us, which was contrary to us, and took it out of the way, nailing it to his cross."

"Judge," I said, "you will understand, of course, that where there is a plain case of guilt and the evidence is undeniable, the only escape for the defendant is that someone will pay the price."

"Yes, I understand that perfectly; but where can I find one who will pay my price?"

"Oh," I replied, "that is the story of the last Scripture we just read. Christ at the cross was paying your price. Because He was a sufficient Savior and was acceptable to God for you, God let Him die for you at Calvary, taking your punishment, bearing your sins, becoming guilty of your wicked ways and evil deeds. There He died in your room and stead that you might go free."

The old gentleman was in a deep study by this time. I could see that his heart was greatly affected by this new revelation of a substitute in the judgment. His eyes were closed under those great bushy eyebrows, and as I placed my hand on his I felt that his body was trembling with emotion. He looked at me shortly, and said, "Did He do that for me, doctor?"

"Yes, judge," I was happy to reply, "He came to seek and to save that which was lost" (Luke 19:10). You are the lost man. It was you He came to save. Will you trust Him to do it?"

With a trembling voice filled with emotion, he answered, "Yes, I will gladly trust Him. I never knew before that God had sent Him to die in my place, to take my punishment, to suffer for me. I thank Him for it. I believe His word. He said it and it must be so."

I knelt beside the chair, holding his hand in mine, and with deep gratitude praised the Savior for His wonderful love, thanked God for His gracious work, and thanked the Holy Spirit for revealing the Savior to this aged sinner who had sought and found the Savior.

Do not wait, my friend, until you are eighty. Trust Christ now! You may never have the opportunity which God gave the old judge at his advanced age. This judge met his Judge, and the records were cleared before the judgment day. You can do this, too!

A Santa Fe Engineer Stopped at the Semaphore

A special meeting was in progress at the Memorial Church, and a great interest had been shone on the part of both the saved and the unsaved in the messages which were being given. One evening, as I came to the church just before the service was to begin, the head usher addressed me at the door and said that an old gentleman, sitting near the front, would like to have a personal conversation before the preaching began.

The usher led me down to the third seat from the front, where I found a tall, straight figure, a man about eighty-one years of age. His solemn face told of the turmoil going on within his heart. The gray hairs and the wrinkles told of a long life of hard labor. He asked for a personal interview immediately, stating: "This matter is too important to delay until the close of the service. I would like to talk with you right now."

Taking the old gentleman by the arm, we went into one of the Sunday school rooms to be alone. The pastor opened the meeting and continued until I was free to come to the platform.

Sitting down, I said to him, "What is your name, and what is your occupation?" Giving his name, he added that for thirty-five years he had been the engineer of a fast passenger train on the Santa Fe running out of Kansas City.

"Has the Lord saved you yet?" I inquired, "or would you like to be?"

The tears coursed down his cheeks as he replied: "I have attended all of your services here and have not been able to sleep or rest, because I realize that the years of my life have been spent for the devil, and I am not ready to die. Will the Lord Jesus save a wicked old man?"

What a joy it was to see the work of the Holy Spirit, convicting this friend of his sinfulness and his need of the Savior. He was deeply in earnest and had prayed that he might know that his sins were forgiven. Opening my Bible to Luke 19:10, we read together: "The Son of man is come to seek and to save that which was lost." We next read I Timothy 1:15, "This is a faithful saying, and worthy of all acceptation, that Christ Jesus came into the world to save sinners."

"You will see from this, my friend," I said, "that the Lord Jesus Christ wants to save you. He has come to do it, He is ready to do it, and He has done all of the necessary work at Calvary in order that He may save you. Because the Lord Jesus must save you in a righteous way, Mr. E——, it was necessary for Him to go to Calvary and suffer for your sins—paying your debt. He did this fully for you, as He says in I Peter 2:24, 'Who his own self bare our sins in his own body on the tree.'"

"Tell me, Mr. E——," I continued, "did you ever run past a red semaphore along the right-of-way?"

He raised himself up straight as an arrow, looked down upon me from his six feet four inches in height, and said with pride: "Young man, I never did. Do you think that the Santa Fe would have kept me in their service on a 'crack' passenger train for thirty-five years if I had ever done such a foolish thing? I never did!"

"No, Mr. E——, I am quite sure they would not, and I well believe that you were a faithful and dependable engineer, following out the rules of the road. Have you been as careful with God as you were with the Santa Fe? He, too, has a semaphore, which He erected along your pathway to eternity. His semaphore has two arms on it. It is the Cross of Christ, and is red with the blood of the Savior. You have perhaps been running past this danger signal all your life. You knew it was there, but perhaps you didn't care. You knew you should stop, but perhaps you were too busy—too occupied with other things.

By this time Mr. E—— was in deep meditation. He sat thinking of his relationship to this Savior and of his neglect through his long life of the One who would have saved him, kept him, and made him fruitful. Since he did not reply to my question, I said to him further: "Will you, just now, stop at that Cross where Jesus died and think of His love for you when He paid the penalty for your sins? He is now in Heaven seated on the throne, watching and waiting to see what you will do with Him, and waiting for you to trust Him. He is not on the Cross now; He is on the throne, and wants you to trust Him, believe in Him, and accept Him. If you will, just now, commit your case, your cause, your sins and yourself to that lovely Savior, He will make you His own child and will blot out every sin."

The engineer arose from his seat, knelt beside the chair, and said with sobs: "Lord Jesus, I believe in You; I want to stop right now beside Your Cross and accept You. You died for me and You live for me, and I trust You with my soul."

I, too, prayed with deep thanksgiving and worshiped the God of Heaven who had brought another wanderer to the fold and pardoned him in the sunset of life. As we came from the little room into the church auditorium, the audience saw the radiance of his face. The wife arose to embrace him with a new joy in her heart.

You, too, my friend, may "Stop, Look, and Listen" at the Cross of Calvary and then turn to Christ in His glory and make Him your own Lord and Savior. Will you do it now?

Is Gertrude First or Jesus?

Gertrude was a precious little girl of eight and one-half years old — the only child of her devoted mother, very attractive in her ways and very beautiful in appearance. She loved the Lord, read often of His love to her in the beautiful new Bible, received as a prize at the Sunday school, was always first in her class for memorizing Bible verses, and devoted to her mother in the home as well.

One day a dreaded disease of childhood struck this beautiful flower, and she was stricken helpless. Day and night the mother and father prayed and watched. They sought the best help obtainable in the medical profession, but it was God's will to take this little one home for Himself to raise instead of these parents. Leaving the little body in its last resting place, the distracted mother left the beautiful home to sorrow alone in her grief at the lake-side resort.

Through the kindness of God, a Bible conference had been planned in the little village where she was resting and she attended the first service. It was arranged to devote this service to questions and answers. We observed a lady in the audience weeping throughout the service, especially when the question touched on death, or the condition of the soul after death.

Immediately after the meeting, the friend departed. However, I made inquiry of the pastor concerning her. He told me the story of her sorrow and heartbreak, after which we

prayed together that our Lord would bring to this troubled
heart His own peace, and give her the garment of praise for the
spirit of heaviness. She returned that evening with others of her
family, and listened very intently as I sought to tell the friends
how the Lord Jesus Christ saves from a life of sin here, and
saves from an eternity of punishment hereafter.

We observed that the message seemed to be taking hold of
her heart, and that there was an attitude of hopefulness and
expectancy which told us that the Holy Spirit was dealing with
her. She remained a while after the evening meeting, so that I
had an opportunity to speak to her personally and to learn a
little of the tragedy which had cast her soul into such darkness.
Before leaving her, I gave her Ephesians 2:14—"For he is our
peace," and said to her, "When you have Him, my friend, you
will have the peace for which your heart craves. His presence,
His Word, His work, all combined, bring peace to the troubled
heart."

The next morning, while sitting at breakfast in the home of
my host, a phone call came from my friend, Mrs. J——, inviting
me to accompany her as she took her father and mother out for
a drive around the lake in her motor car. "I want to tell you all
that is in my heart," she said, "so that you may really help me
to find the Lord." It was only a little while before she drove up
to the house. She was weeping when I entered the car, and as
we drove out of the village into the country, she told me the
story of her loss and sorrow. "I know I am a lost sinner," she
said, "because last night in the service you said: 'Those who
belong to Christ want to see their Savior first of all. They will
not put their relatives first, no matter how near and dear they
may be. Christ will be first to occupy the heart's attention when
the soul goes home to glory.' Immediately my heart said: 'I do
not want to see Jesus first of all; I want to see my Gertrude. I
want to go to Heaven to see Gertrude, not to see Jesus.' That
thought, doctor, and the terrible sinfulness of it, crowded out
my sleep last night, and I was forced to rise and walk the floor
in agony of spirit, because I knew then that Jesus meant very
little to me. I became fully persuaded then that I was a lost
sinner with no Savior. This thought has filled my soul with
deep sorrow. I must find Him."

Throughout the next two hours, as we were driving along,
I called attention to many Gospel verses, dwelling on each one

and explaining the work of the Lord Jesus and His love for her. None of these words, however, gave her any peace. She returned for the evening service, and the message for the night was on John 10:9 — "I am the door: by me if any man enter in, he shall be saved, and shall go in and out, and find pasture." I stressed the point of coming personally by faith to the living Lord on the throne and committing the whole soul, sin, and life to Him. I pressed home the attitude of heart found in those beautiful words: "Lord, I believe."

This message seemed to take hold of the heart of my sorrowing friend. She left the church without fully trusting Christ, but with an attitude of seeking Him. The next morning, about nine o'clock, the telephone rang again, and I heard this joyful message: "At midnight, I knelt at my bedside, and said, 'Lord Jesus, you are more to me than Gertrude. You gave your life for me; you came to save me. You have promised to take me to the Father, and I trust you; I believe in you.' I am saved, doctor. I want to see my Savior first of all." Thus does our Lord bind up the broken heart and heal the wounds of life.

Several letters have been received from this friend, all of them telling the same story of peace and joy in Christ, and a soul resting in His eternal love. Whom do you want to see FIRST of all?

Little Joe with a Big Question

Located in the hills of Missouri is a typical country schoolhouse, not at all attractive in appearance, nor situated on a modern highway. In this little, obscure place, however, there was one evening a great transaction which changed the life of one fine lad of twelve, and through him, of many others.

I had the joy of presenting to this group the Gospel as it is found in Romans 10:9—"If thou shalt confess with thy mouth the Lord Jesus, and shalt believe in thine heart that God hath raised Him from the dead, thou shalt be saved." A number of illustrations were used in order to explain the meaning of the confession mentioned in this verse. The policeman, wearing his blue uniform and showing the star on his breast, is thus making a confession of his connection with the police department and the authority vested in him as an officer of the law. The bank messenger, with his blue uniform and the name of the bank on his cap, is confessing by these that he is employed by the great bank in the heart of the city. The soldier in his khaki uniform, with the marks on the collar, is confessing that he has entered the service of his country and is no longer his own master, but is governed entirely by the will and the law of his superior officers.

Near the back of the room in this little schoolhouse, sat a boy twelve years of age with tousled hair, and wearing a soiled torn pair of overalls. One could easily see that he came from a family which had been denied the luxuries of life and many of the necessities. In his home were eleven other children, and the father worked on the section along the railroad. All through the service this lad listened closely and attentively. He had never heard a message like that before. There was a tug at his little heart as he heard the story of the Savior calling and inviting boys and girls, men, and women to come and put their trust under the shadow of His wings.

At the close of the meeting, the little lad elbowed his way through the crowded aisle toward the front. He dodged under the arms and between the bodies of the folk who crowded the little room, until he came to where I was standing. Looking up at me with an eager face and attractive countenance, he said: "Mister, how old does a boy have to be to be saved?"

What a question is this? Many older ones have asked it. Sunday school teachers have pondered over it. Parents have inquired concerning it; but never before had I been asked about it by a child. Praying quickly for wisdom, I slipped one arm around his shoulders, and said: "My little friend, you must be just old enough to know that the Lord Jesus came to save you, and to tell Him that He can have you to be His own. Would you like to tell Him so?"

He bowed his head for a few moments in meditation and then looking up with a sweet smile, said: "Yes, Mister, I'll take Jesus right now." That was all! Others crowded up to converse and he was soon lost in the crowd.

Later on, I learned his name and made some inquiries about little Joe, and whether he really was walking with the Lord and trusting this new-found Savior. The report came back: "Yes, Joe is really saved. Someone has given him a Bible. He carries it to school with him. He has it on his desk with his other books. At recess when the boys are playing their games, Joe is sitting in the grass over by the fence, reading his Bible and meditating on the precious Lord and Savior he has found."

Joe is still carrying his Bible, though several years have passed. He has learned to know the Gospel so well that he is able to tell it to others publicly and privately, and has proven by his godly life that on that eventful day, he really did take the Lord Jesus Christ for himself and the blessed Savior took him to be His very own.

A boy of twelve is not too young to be saved, nor is he too young to be lost. I trust that every boy and girl who reads this beautiful story may do as Joe did, and say at once: "I will take God's gift; I will receive the Lord Jesus, for He died for me."

A Troubled Pool
Found Peace

The village of T—— is a quiet little spot on the Missouri River, surrounded on three sides by hills. In this district there resided many country folk who had heard and learned to love the Gospel.

One day, I received a call from these friends to spend the following Sunday with them. Having an open date, I was glad to go and thus take advantage of the opportunity to minister to those who did not possess very much in the way of earthly goods.

Arriving at the depot, I was met by the station agent who at once extended a very cordial invitation to have lunch at their modest little home about two and one-half miles up in the hills on a winding dirt road. I gladly accepted the invitation so that I might have a visit with these friends who were actively seeking to spread the Gospel in their narrow sphere.

On the way out to the home, my hostess explained that the real reason for requesting this visit was that I might help a carpenter, who happened at that time to be working on their house, making a few repairs. She had been giving the Gospel story to this neighbor and he seemed to be quite interested, but could not find his way to the Savior. The path was not clear and the Gospel was not fully understood.

We reached the little cottage just before noon, and found a nice warm fire burning in the sitting room stove. I was urged to make myself at home, while my friend went to the kitchen to see how the mother was progressing with lunch. Meantime, I stood near the stove to gain more advantage of its warmth and was praying that the Lord might give some message that would help the carpenter.

When my hostess returned to the room, the carpenter followed her. She introduced him by saying: "Doctor, this is Mr. Pool, the carpenter, who is making repairs on our home. Mr. Pool, this is Dr. Wilson."

We shook hands cordially, and I said to him: "I am so happy to meet you, Mr. Pool, for I read in the Bible about a 'pool' that was troubled by the Lord."

"My!" he exclaimed, "that is strange, for I'm that fellow, but I didn't know it was in the Bible; tell me about it."

Sitting down with him beside the stove, I said: "Mr. Pool, has the Lord been troubling you about your sins and your soul?"

"Yes," he replied, "very much. For the last several months I have been troubled about the matter, and would like to know how to get peace with God."

I soon had my Bible open to the fifth chapter of John, where we read the story of the impotent man lying helpless beside the pool. At certain times an angel of the Lord came down and troubled the waters of the pool. The helpless cripple said: "Sir, I have no man, when the water is troubled, to put me into the pool. . . . Jesus saith unto him, Rise, take up thy bed, and walk." Immediately the man was healed, and found the peace and blessing which his heart had been wanting for thirty-eight years.

"You see, Mr. Pool," I said, "all that was necessary there was a meeting between the suffering sinner and the sufficient Savior. You need Him, too, Mr. Pool. He came to put away your sins. 'The Son of man is come to seek and to save that which was lost' (Luke 19:10). You are the lost man and the Savior came for you. 'He that believeth on the Son hath everlasting life' (John 3:36). And again, Mr. Pool, look at this verse, John 1:12—'But as many as received him, to them gave he power to become the sons of God, even to them that believe on his name.' If you will take Him right now to be the Lord of your life and the Savior of your soul, you will be His, Mr. Pool, and He will be yours. If you consider yourself to be an ungodly man, then hear this Scripture: 'Christ died for the ungodly' (Romans 5:6)."

Mr. Pool arose slowly from the chair, walked over to the window, looked out upon a large pasture, and there with folded arms, he was in meditation for some moments. After a while, he turned about and said to me: "Doctor, I believe that Christ Jesus came to save sinners and to save me. I accept Him as my own Lord and Savior. I believe He blotted out my sins when He died for me, and that I am saved today because I have accepted Him."

We knelt together beside the chair and there with thankful hearts praised the God of all grace for His gift of such a wonderful Savior. We praised the Savior Himself, who had given His life to bring peace to this troubled POOL. We worshipped together the One who had made us both children of God by His sovereign grace and saving power.

When my hostess returned to the room, she saw at once the joy and peace that illuminated the face of her carpenter friend, and joined with us in a season of rejoicing. You, too, my friend, may find this same Savior if you will accept Him and trust Him.

He will blot out your sins and make you His own forever.

An Unusual
Pullman Experience

Not long since, I had occasion to make a trip from St. Louis to New York. Being rather a long journey, I desired to obtain a lower berth, which to my mind offered the greater comfort and rest. However, to my dismay, I was obliged to take an upper, as the lowers, unfortunately, had all been taken. The berth just beneath mine was occupied by a young Italian mother with two babies—one of them about six months old and the other about two and a half years.

As the train pulled out of the station, I took from my case a Bible bound in pig-skin leather of an unusual color. Having read passage after passage, I noticed that the young woman was watching me closely and apparently with a great deal of interest. This curiosity continued to increase, until she addressed me, saying: "Pardon me, sir; what strange book is that which you are reading? I have never seen one that looked like that in my life."

"This is a Bible. It is God's precious Word and is a wonderfully fine book to read."

"What a strange title for a book," she exclaimed. "What is the story about, and who is the author?"

This unusual lack of knowledge of the Bible was a great surprise to me, and I quickly slipped a prayer to Heaven for guidance, saying: "God is the author of this book, the Holy Spirit wrote it as He inspired holy men of God, and the story is largely about you. Did you never see this book, nor hear about it from any one?"

"No," she replied, "I never did."

"Where were you raised?" I then asked. "Were you never in church?"

"I was born in Italy," she said, "and was brought to this country when I was about one year old. None of my people here ever went to church, and I was never in a church of any kind. I would like to know about that book, though, and what it says about me. May I look at it with you?"

"Most certainly," I said, eager to help her. Upon receiving this reply, she called for the porter, requested two pillows which she placed on the seat in front of the babies to keep them from falling off, while she sat beside me on the other seat.

As this change was being made, and taking advantage of the opportunity, I said to her: "This book was written by the saints. Did you ever hear of them?"

"Oh, yes," she answered, "they were great people and knew many things about God and the angels, but I did not know that they knew anything about me; and I certainly did not know that they had written anything about me."

She took her seat beside me, and I pointed out to her the names at the top of the pages: "Saint" Paul, "Saint" John, "Saint" Luke, "Saint" Peter, and the others. This brought a feeling of expectancy and hopefulness into the heart of the young woman, who felt that whatever the saints said surely must be true. "What did they write about me?" again she asked.

"Let me show you," said I, and turned at once to Romans 3:9-19. The passage referred to reads (in part) as follows: "There is none righteous, no, not one; there is none that understandeth, there is none that seeketh after God. . . . Whose mouth is full of cursing and bitterness; . . . destruction and misery are in their ways." After reading the entire passage, this young mother was trembling and perspiring, and showed evidences of a very deep conviction of sin. "My!" she said, "that's terrible. The worst of it, Mister, that it's all true; but I never dreamed that the saints knew it and had written it all out in this strange book. Please do not read any more to me about that. Do tell me how to escape from the results of it. It there any remedy? Is there any forgiveness?"

The Lord very quickly had revealed to this young mother her true state in His sight and her condition before Him. She had accepted the accusation and denied nothing. She believed God's Word and received the indictment as being true. Of course it was not necessary to go further with this line of reading, therefore I turned at once to Isaiah 53:5-6. We read it together—"But he was wounded for our transgressions, he was bruised for our iniquities; the chastisement of our peace was upon him; and with his stripes we are healed. All we like sheep have gone astray; we have turned every one to his own way; and the Lord hath laid on him the iniquity of us all."

"Who was suffering so?" she inquired. "Whose iniquities were laid on Him?"

Replying to this, I turned to I Timothy 1:15 and read— "'This is a faithful saying, and worthy of all acceptation [worthy of you accepting it, lady], that Christ Jesus came into the world to save sinners' The One who suffered was the Savior; the one that He suffered for was you."

"But how do I know it was for me?"

"Because you are the sinner, are you not?"

"Oh, yes. I am a terrible sinner, and I do need someone to put away my sins."

"Christ came to do that," I said. "We will see. In Hebrews 9:26, we read: 'But now once in the end of the world hath he appeared to put away sin by the sacrifice of himself.'"

"How can all this be mine?" she asked, earnestly and with deep emotion. Turning the pages to John 3:16, together we read that beautiful passage—"For God so loved the world, that he gave his only begotten Son, that whosoever believeth in him should not perish, but have everlasting life."

"Will you now believe in the Lord Jesus, that He came to save you, that He suffered for your sins, and that you may accept Him as God's gift to you?"

"Yes, indeed, I do take Him right now. Oh, how glad I am that He suffered for my sins. I do accept Him as my own Savior."

It was now the noon hour, and the dinner call had come from the dining car. The little mother took her two babies away for their lunch, and shortly after I followed—but not to the same table. When we returned to our seats, the mother again placed the pillows in front of the babies, sat down beside me, and said: "Please tell me some more about Jesus. He must have loved me very much to make Him willing to die for me."

The passage chosen was Acts 9:26-40. This is the story of the eunuch riding along in his chariot reading Isaiah 53:5-6. Phillip came by the direction of the Holy Spirit, explained the passage, and the eunuch trusted Christ and was saved. After reading through the story carefully, with such explanations as seemed helpful, the new convert exclaimed, "How wonderful it is that this man and myself should have such a similar experience! He was riding in his chariot and I on this train. Phillip came with a Bible and you came with yours. Phillip read in Isaiah 53 about the sufferings of Christ, and that is the passage you read to me. This man believed the message and accepted Jesus, and so have I accepted Him. I do wish there was some water here, so that I, too, could be baptized. I want to go all the way with the Savior."

Before parting, I promised to send a nice new Bible to this newborn child of God, so that she might read for herself the wonderful story of this wonderful Savior. This I did upon reaching New York. Have you met Christ Jesus the Savior? Be sure that in the maze of your religious experiences you do not miss meeting and trusting Him for yourself.

The Preacher Found Christ

Occasionally, the call of the pulpit reaches the mind and heart of an unsaved young man, who sees in that work a great opportunity for helpful service. He enters a seminary, studies the Bible and allied subjects for four years, is graduated and receives a "charge" in some city or village where he begins his public ministry. Such was the case of a minister about forty years of age, who visited me in my office one Monday morning about ten o'clock.

A Christian friend had driven many miles from a neighboring city to bring his pastor to see me. All night long, the pastor had walked the floor, read the Word, prayed, and conversed with my farmer friend concerning his own need of meeting Christ. He was introduced to me as the Rev. Mr. C—— from G—— City. After the introduction, my friend left and we two were together in my office with the Bible and the Lord.

"Tell me about yourself," I said, "so that I may know what line of thought to pursue, in seeking to help you."

"I am pastor of the C—— Church in G—— City, where I have been now for four years. Altogether, I have been in the ministry for fourteen years. I graduated from the seminary and have never been without a pulpit since that time."

"About six months ago," he continued, "I began to search my heart to see why there were so few conversions under my ministry, and why it seemed so difficult for me to pray. The more I looked into the experiences of my heart during the past twenty years, the darker I seemed to get in my soul. I wrote to my superintendent about my distress, and he replied that I was simply restless in my spirit, because I did not have enough to do. He suggested that I should begin a building program and get rid of the old structure which was very old, dusty, and dirty, and build an attractive new place."

"Was this the case?" I asked. "Do you think that a new building would give you peace?"

"No, certainly not," he answered, "and I wrote at once to my superintendent, telling him that what I needed was not activity, nor a new building, but a new experience in my heart. I received no reply to that letter."

"The reason I have now come to you is this: Last night, at the close of the service in my church, one of my church officers came to me, and said, 'Pastor, why is it that when you preach nothing happens? You have been with us now for several years, but we see no tears in the audience, no broken hearts over sin, and really you do not teach very much of the Scriptures. What is wrong?'"

"I felt that I had kept up my hypocrisy too long and should not continue it another day. 'My brother, it is because it has never happened to me,' I answered him. 'I have never been really converted myself. This has been a burden on my heart for some months, and I give you my word that I will never again preach in this pulpit, or any other, until I have found Christ for myself and experienced in my own soul that change of heart which I have been preaching about to others, with so little success.' That, doctor, is why I am here to see you this morning."

This confession from my friend at once presented to me a difficult problem. Here was a man who knew the Bible fairly well, had received four years of training in the study of it, had preached on its texts for fourteen years, and still was in profound darkness and ignorant of the way of salvation?

"How shall I begin with you?" I asked. "You are well acquainted with the Bible."

"Just begin with me," he said, "as you would with a heathen. Just forget that I know anything at all about the Bible and start right at the beginning of the Gospel story. As you tell it to me, I will find where I have missed the way; so just start in."

"We will begin our conversation," I said, "by seeing your need of this Savior. Let us read God's indictment in Romans 3:9-19: 'What then? are we better than they? No, in no wise: for we have before proved both Jews and Gentiles, that they are all under sin; As it is written, There is none righteous, no, not one: There is none that understandeth, there is none that seeketh after God. They are all gone out of the way, they are together become unprofitable; there is none that doeth good, no, not one. Their throat is an open sepulchre; with their tongues they have used deceit; the poison of asps is under their lips: Whose mouth is full of cursing and bitterness: Their feet are swift to shed blood: Destruction and misery are in their ways: And the way of peace have they not known: There is no fear of God before their eyes. Now we know that what things soever the law saith, it saith to them who are under the law: that every mouth may be stopped, and all the world may become guilty before God.'"

We read the passage through carefully. After each verse I asked him, "Is this true of you? Is this what the Lord thinks of you?" We spent quite a little time on those verses because his heart until then was really not ready to admit that he was that bad.

"This is not what I think of you, my friend, it is what God thinks of you. If God, in His love, tells us what He sees in our hearts, we should bow to it. We should not set our judgment of ourselves in opposition to God's revealed judgment of us."

"No," he said, "that is right, and though I had not thought until now that I was that bad, I accept His accusation and confess my guilt."

We next turned to Romans 5:6, which reads, "When we were yet without strength, in due time Christ died for the ungodly."

"Are you helpless," I asked him, "and are you the ungodly one—quite unable to help yourself?"

"Yes, that describes me," he answered. "I know that only the Savior can save, and I want Him to save me this morning."

We next read "For God so loved the world that he gave his only begotten Son, that whosoever believeth in him, should not perish, but have everlasting life" (John 3:16), and "Verily, verily, I say unto you, He that heareth my word, and believeth on him that sent me, hath everlasting life, and shall not come into condemnation; but is passed from death unto life" (John 5:24). Both of these verses were explained to my preacher friend in some detail. The explanations did not bring light to his heart, nor peace. His countenance remained sad.

The Holy Spirit was working in his heart, and we realized His blessed presence. I quickly prayed to Him for wisdom and guidance, and then turned to John 1:12, where we read together this passage: "But as many as received him, to them gave He power to become the Sons of God, even to them that believe on his name." With this verse we joined I John 5:12, where it is recorded: "He that hath the Son hath life; and he that hath not the Son of God hath not life."

These two Scriptures were used of the Lord to bring the light to his darkened heart. "That," said he, "is the very place where I have missed being a Christian. I have read about Christ and believed what I read. I have preached about Christ and believed what I preached, but I have never made Him my own. There never was a time when I went to Christ Jesus personally and told Him that I would take Him as my Lord and Savior. But I will accept Him just now. He knows that my heart is hungry and I believe His Word which says: 'Him that cometh to me I will in no wise cast out'" (John 6:37).

Two years later, when I met this pastor again in a different city at a Christian Endeavor Conference, he greeted me with unusual affection and said: "Not only do I have the peace with God myself, but the Lord is now saving souls through my ministry constantly."

Are you, my friend, seeking to preach or teach without first having been saved yourself? Do take Jesus Christ NOW. He will save you and you will be His own child.

He Brought His Night-Shirt

In a lovely little city in the heart of Kansas, a group of Christians rented an abandoned theatre for a series of Gospel meetings, and invited me to conduct the services. The meetings were advertised in surrounding towns and a goodly company of interested folk gathered to hear the Gospel.

The leader of this work was standing at the front of the theatre, near the platform, talking to me about the arrangements, just before the service was to begin. We observed a man about fifty years of age walking down the aisle carrying a suitcase. Approaching us, he placed his suitcase on the floor, and then asked, "Where can I see the evangelist?"

My friend said: "This is the preacher who will conduct the services. You may talk with him now if you wish."

I immediately shook hands with the visitor and inquired how I might help him. "I came to be saved," he said. "I have been playing at this business for many years and am now fifty years old. It is time I got it settled. I drove thirty miles to come to this meeting to hear you and I hope you will explain it to me fully."

"Why did you bring the suitcase?" I asked.

"I brought my night-shirt in it, because I expect to stay here until I get saved. I am not going home until I know that I am a real Christian."

It is not often that we see such interest manifested as this. Such determination and purpose of heart will always be blessed by the Lord. I felt confident that the Holy Spirit would reveal the Lord Jesus Christ to this man because of his seeking and his coming. The Lord said: "Those that seek me early shall find me."

We sat down together, occupying seats in the front row, and I said to him: "What part of the Scriptures do you know the best?"

"I only know John 3:16," he replied.

"That is a splendid verse," I remarked. "I wonder if you believe what it says?"

"Of course I do," he said, "every word of it."

"Will you quote it for me?"

"Yes, gladly," he answered, and repeated: "For God so loved the world that he gave his only begotten Son, that whosoever believeth in him should not perish, but have everlasting life."

"Since you tell me that you believe this verse, my friend, will you kneel here with me and thank God for several things which I will enumerate to you?"

"Yes," he said, "I am willing to do anything at all that I should do in order to be saved. That is what I came for; that is my only desire."

"Very well," said I, "let us kneel together and I will ask you to thank God first for giving His Son to you. Will you do this?"

"Yes," he said.

"Next I will ask you to tell God that you accept this gift and receive His Son to be your own Lord and Savior. Will you do this, as you tell Him?"

"I certainly will," he replied.

"The third thing is to thank God for giving you everlasting life, right now, just where you are, because you have taken His own Son for yourself. Will you thank Him for this, too?"

"Yes, I will be glad to do it," he answered.

"Also, I will ask you to thank the Lord that you will never perish, never be lost, never go to hell, because you believe that Jesus Christ, the Lord of glory, blotted out your sins at Calvary."

"Yes, I will tell Him that right away," was his answer.

"Now, my friend, will you turn your heart to the One who sits at God's right hand on the throne, the wounded Savior, and say to Him: 'Lord Jesus, I thank Thee for dying for me on the cross. I believe that You bore my sins there and that You blotted them out. I thank You for it, I worship You, and I trust You with my soul?'"

"Yes," he replied quickly, "I will do all that you have told me, for I do want to get peace in my heart."

We then knelt together, and he began to pray. In his prayer, he said: "O God, I thank Thee for sending Jesus into the world to save the world. O God, won't you make me a good Christian. O God, won't you give me peace and help me to live a good life. O God do —."

Just there I reached over, shook his shoulder sharply, and said: "Stop! there is no use of your praying like that; you are just wasting your time as well as God's time."

He turned about quite frightened, arose from his knees, and trembling with emotion, said, "What's the matter; what was I doing wrong?"

"You did not do any one of the five things which I asked you to do," I explained to him. "You did not thank God for giving His Son to you. You did not tell God that you here and now accepted this gift; neither did you thank the Lord for the gift of eternal life. You said nothing about the joy of knowing that you would never perish. You completely ignored the Lord Jesus, and said nothing to Him whatever about the wonderful work He did for you at Calvary. You must accept God's Christ if you would be God's child. You need not ask God to do anything for you; it has already been done. The gift has already been given; the sacrifice has already been made; the blood has already been shed. God wants you to believe it and to accept this Savior just now. Will you do it?"

"Yes," he said, "I will pray again."

We again knelt down together as he prayed again, and said: "O God, since talking with the doctor, I see I told you the wrong thing. O God, I do take your Son right now. I do accept your gift to me, and I believe that He came to save me; and O God, I believe that you have given me eternal life this afternoon. Thank you, O God, I thank you I will never perish. Oh, I thank you for the wonderful peace you have given me. Lord Jesus, I thank you for taking away all of my sins and blotting them out with your blood. You have saved me; I worship you; I believe you."

Thus he poured out his heart in gratitude, and arose with such thanksgiving and praise that the friends who were gathering for the service were deeply impressed with the blessing that God had given him.

Each one who reads this story is urged to make Christ Jesus your own Lord and Savior; trust Him with your soul and lay at His feet your life. He will save you, keep you, and use you.

The Worst Woman in the Church

Sunday night had come, and the meetings which had been widely advertised were ready for the opening service. The church was crowded. Even the platform, the stairs, and the aisles were filled to capacity. The choir was in its place, the leader of song was on the platform, and the pianist seated at the piano. As I sat beside the pastor on the platform, my attention was attracted to the lady at the piano because of her distinguished appearance, and the evidences of culture and wealth which she presented.

The first hymn was announced, and as the beautiful song was played, I noted that the pianist was one of no mean ability.

"Who is the lady at the piano?" I asked the pastor.

"The worst woman in the church," he said. "She certainly causes me more trouble than any other person, and I wish she were not here in this meeting."

I was not expecting such a reply as this concerning one who seemed to be so able and so attractive. Continuing my question, I asked, "What is the trouble? In what way does she disturb you?"

He answered quickly: "Being a prominent woman in our city, she exerts a great influence on the people of this church."

I could readily see that the woman could do either a great deal of good or harm by her leadership. He continued: "This lady teaches one of the classes in our Sunday school, — a class of young matrons. She leaves the church after teaching her class and does not attend the church service, but goes to the theatre, enjoys card parties, and is just as much interested in worldly things as in spiritual, and even more so. She is a bad example to all the members of this flock. I can do nothing with her. She will not listen to counsel."

It seemed quite a sad situation to me and so I suggested to the pastor that we slip into his study while the preliminary song service was continuing so that there we might pray together for this leading lady.

"No, I do not care to go," the pastor said. "I have prayed for her and with her; I have pleaded and argued. I have preached against worldliness in her presence, but none of these things touch her, nor change her. I wish she were not in the service at all."

"Is it possible," said I, "that there is a lost soul in this congregation who should not be here — one who is so hardened that even the living Christ cannot reach her heart? I will go and pray that she may be the first one to be saved."

The pastor's study was quite handy, so I slipped in alone to plead with the Lord that He would make the "worst woman in the church" the very best. When I returned to the platform, it was time for my ministry to begin. I observed that the pianist was forced to remain on the bench, because there were no seats available. Every place was filled. For the first fifteen minutes of the message she paid little or no attention. She had been to many meetings and listened to much preaching, and rather considered that none of it was of interest to her.

The message that evening was an exposition of the Gospel. I sought to tell the story from the Gospel of John of the value of the Lord Jesus Christ to the needy soul. A story caught her fancy and attracted her attention. The illustration seemed to appeal to her, and throughout the remainder of the service she listened attentively. I was especially stressing John 3:36 — "He that believeth not the Son shall not see life, but the wrath of God abideth on him." I mentioned that it was possible to believe very much about the Son without believing on the Son Himself; that it was possible to believe the facts without accepting and appropriating them.

At the close of the serve, our friend left the church without speaking to the pastor or to the evangelist. We wondered if she would return. She did return Monday night and requested one of the ushers to save her a seat in the middle of the front row. After the song service was ended, she came over and sat down immediately in front of me and listened closely to the message on "Justification." The text was Romans 5:1 — "Therefore being justified by faith, we have peace with God through our Lord Jesus Christ." To this text was added the ninth verse — "Much more than, being now justified by his blood, we shall be saved from wrath through him."

This message evidently deepened the work of the night before. She listened closely all through the service, and at the close shook hands with the speaker, but did not wait for a personal conversation. With the soul stirred, she returned Tuesday night and again requested that a seat be reserved for her as before. The message was given on Ephesians 2:8-9 — "For by grace are ye saved through faith; and that not of yourselves: it is the gift of God: not of works, lest any man should boast." Her deep interest was quite manifest now, and she did not lose a single word of the message.

Wednesday night arrived, and by that time the pastor saw the great change which had taken place in her attitude, and observed that she was following the message closely; so now he was happy to join me in prayer that Wednesday night might be the night of decision. Our friend did not leave the piano that evening, for some one had taken the seat she had reserved and there was no other place to go. After I had spoken a few moments, she dropped her head in her hands and did not again look up throughout the service. The Lord was working in her heart. Some on the platform were praying while I was preaching.

At the close of the service, I hurried to her side — for she was still sitting at the piano, and I found she was weeping.

"May I help you?" I asked kindly.

"Yes," she said, "I am a hypocrite and a terrible sinner, and I would like to have peace in my soul from God."

It was not possible, in the midst of the crowd, to have a quiet, personal talk with her, so I took out a card and wrote on it three Scriptures — John 3:36; John 1:12; and I John 5:12. Handing it to her, I said: "Please read these when you go home in the order in which I have written them. The first Scripture tells you of God's gift, the second one tells you to accept the gift, while the third one tells you the blessing that results from accepting the gift. Please read these on your knees alone with God, and then tell me tomorrow night whether you have accepted Jesus Christ and whether He is now your Lord and Savior."

"He that believeth on the Son hath everlasting life: and he that believeth not the Son shall not see life; but the wrath of God abideth on him." (John 3:36)

"But as many as received him, to them gave He power to become the sons of God, even to them that believe on his name." (John 1:12)

"He that hath the Son hath life; and he that hath not the Son of God hath not life." (I John 5:12)

We prayed much that evening that the Word of God would be effective in her heart. When she returned Thursday night and took her place at the piano, we could see a wonderful change had been wrought in her heart. The radiant face, the buoyant step, the joy in the playing, all told the story in no uncertain terms. At the close of the service, she hurried to us to tell how, in the upper room at home, she had turned her heart and soul to Christ, and had within her heart the "peace which passeth understanding."

Are you active in the church, my friend, and yet a hindrance? Are you a professing Christian without having Christ? Are you busy in the service of the King without being the child of the King? Do come to that Savior now and He will save you to the uttermost.

The Only "Forgotten" Son

The Holy Spirit wonderfully overrules mistakes when He is dealing with hearts and souls. This was remarkably demonstrated in a meeting which I held in southern Missouri.

At the close of the afternoon service, a young woman with her two children remained seated, waiting for someone to help her in her personal soul-problem. I approached her with the question: "Would you like some help from the Scriptures? Did you understand the message of the afternoon?"

"I would like to be helped," she said. "I remained for that purpose. I do not understand the Bible, and do not know how to be a Christian. Have you time to show me?"

This cordial invitation convinced me that the Lord was dealing with the heart of this young mother, so I sat down beside her with my Bible, and asked, "Is there any part of the Scripture that you can quote?"

"Yes," she said, "I can quote John 3:16, for I learned it in Sunday school."

"Do you understand the meaning of that precious verse?" I inquired.

"No, I really do not. Will you please explain it to me?"

"Yes," I replied, "if you will first quote it."

The quotation which she gave was as follows: "For God so loved the world, that he gave his only 'forgotten' Son, that whosoever believeth in him should not perish, but have everlasting life."

Noticing that she had used the word "forgotten" instead of the word "begotten," I took advantage of the thought in the word, and said: "Do you know why God 'forgot' His Son?"

"No, I do not," she answered. "I have often wondered why."

"It was because the Lord wanted to remember you," I answered. "God in Heaven was willing to part with His Son for a little while, so that He might have you forever. He let His Son be enveloped in terrible darkness, so that He might give you a crown of light. He let Jesus die, so that He could give you eternal life. It was for you, my friend, that God 'forgot' His Son." One could plainly observe that this answer had brought an entirely new thought to the mind and heart of this inquirer. She seemed puzzled for a while. The wonderful truth of the substitution of Christ for her seemed more than she could grasp or accept. We remained quiet for a little while, as she was thinking the matter through, and then she broke the silence by asking: "How do I know that He was doing that for me?"

This question puzzles many hearts. It is a stumbling block to many who attend revival meetings, who have their hearts stirred, and then fail to personally appropriate the Lord and Savior for themselves. The devil usually suggests to the troubled heart that the Gospel is for someone else, and that the Savior is not particularly for him or her.

I replied to her inquiry by reading Romans 5:6 — "For when we were yet without strength, in due time Christ died for the ungodly." Then I said to her, "If you feel and realize that you are among the ungodly, then you may appropriate this remedy for yourself, just as you appropriated this seat for yourself when you entered the church. When you enter a drug store, you realize that the remedies there are for everyone; your own need leads you to take some of it for yourself. When you enter a grocery store, you realize that the food which is there is for everyone; but your hunger leads you to purchase some for yourself. At the street corner, you wait for the bus, realizing that the bus is for every one; but it will only take you down town if you appropriate the bus and a seat for yourself."

These illustrations seemed to clear up her question as to whether Christ was for her alone. I could see that the truth was dawning on her heart and that she was now ready to make Him her own.

"Have you ever noticed, my friend, that it takes two to make a gift?" I asked. "There must be the giver, and there must also be the one who accepts the gift. God has given His Son to you. Now he waits for you to receive His Son. Notice this verse: John 1:12—'But as many as received him, to them gave he power to become the sons of God, even to them that believe on his name.' He wants you to accept that blessed gift right now where you are sitting. When you take Him, He takes you; He becomes your Lord and Savior, and you become His child and His servant."

Eagerly she leaned forward, and said, "Doctor, I will take Him; I want Him. I do take Him just now, and I am sure that He takes me."

The surge of the new-found joy overcame her composure, and she bent her head while she wept quietly a few moments in the presence of her Lord. Then we kneeled together as we poured out our hearts in thanksgiving to the God of Love who gave her everlasting life.

At the evening service she returned and brought her husband, who was an atheist, scoffer and an enemy of the truth. Her testimony to him, and the great change in her attitude toward him, had deeply impressed his heart, and so he came, willing to listen to the message himself.

You, too, will be a soul winner and a blessed example to others, if you will accept Jesus Christ and let Him be the Lord of your life and the Savior of your soul.

The Police Officer Took the Wrong Hat

It is customary for the friends who visit the studios of our radio station to present themselves before the program begins, in order that the speaker may introduce those present. Upon one occasion, after the morning Bible lesson had already begun on the air, a police officer entered the studio. Being a very large man, possibly six foot four inches tall, his uniform accentuated his size. Listening very intently throughout the entire service, he introduced himself at the close as Officer Clark, mentioning that when he was off duty, he enjoyed listening to various radio programs, and particularly the morning Bible lesson.

Shortly after he departed, I approached the rack to get my hat, and noticed that it was gone and another left in its place. It then occurred to me that the officer, who was wearing a soft Fedora hat when he came to the studio, had undoubtedly, in his haste, took mine, which closely resembled his. The hat left for me was much too large for my head, and caused me to present a grotesque appearance as I walked down the street. This aroused not a little curiosity among my friends and drew forth a number of questions.

The following morning, proceeding my Bible lessons on the radio, I requested the police department and the chief of detectives to please institute a search for the officer who took away my hat and left his own, which was much too large for me.

Mr. Clark was at home, listening to the message. At once he called to his wife, and said, "Nellie, will you please go to the hat-rack and see whether I have my own hat or some other? The radio preacher is sending out a call for his hat and I rather think that I am the guilty man."

She soon called back to him, and said, "There is a hat here which does not belong to you. You must have taken it by mistake."

Officer Clark than explained to his wife that all day long this hat felt rather strange on his head, and did not seem to fit as it should. It seemed that he was on night duty, and so during the daytime only he wore his soft hat. He had just returned from his night service, and had sat down to get the morning Bible lesson before retiring for his rest.

The radio message that morning was on the text: "Thou shalt not steal." I sought to impress upon the hearers the fact that we might steal many things from God, which in ordinary life are overlooked. The soul that should belong to Him is kept from Him for personal gain and personal pleasure. The life that should be laid at His feet is devoted to a vain and fruitless search for profit and happiness without Him. The talents and gifts which should be used for the glory of God are used to promote personal aims and ends.

As the officer listened, his mind traveled over a life of some fifty-five years spent for the world, the flesh, and the devil. The Lord had received none of his time nor his money. His talents and energies had been expended for personal gain, and he had sought in every way to add to his pleasure and to increase his wealth. None of these plans, however, had been very successful, and now at the age of sixty-five, he found himself with a job, but with very little else.

The next morning, the officer presented himself at the studio rather early. He wanted to hear more of the message which had so deeply touched his heart. The lesson on this occasion concerned the confession of Christ before men. I used the illustration of the police officer, who by wearing his uniform and badge, was daily confessing his position as a member of the department of justice. Everywhere he went, he was consciously and unconsciously telling the people what his position was and whom he served.

I also used the illustration of the soldier, who in his uniform bearing certain insignia, daily and constantly confessed in that way that he was no longer a free man, but had given himself entirely to the military department of his government. So the Christian, accepting Jesus Christ and putting on Jesus Christ, takes his place as a lover of the Savior and one who has abandoned himself to the Son of God and to the service of the King.

This message stirred the heart of Officer Clark, clearing up in his mind some of the things which had been troubling him. He saw that salvation was not a religion, nor a system of good works. He realized for the first time that he was completely outside the family of God, as he had never yet confessed his faith and his confidence in Jesus Christ.

I sought to lead him to a decision just then in the radio room. It seemed, however, that he was not ready; therefore I seemingly failed in my effort. He left the studio, greatly troubled in soul and with a very heavy heart. Several days later, I rejoiced as I saw the officer entering the studio again, his happy countenance telling the story of a happier heart. After exchanging greetings, he related to me the following experience.

"After leaving you the other morning, I went home, ate breakfast and then went to my room. The Bible was a rather strange book to me, for I had never read it, and I had quite a little difficulty finding the Scriptures you used. I read a great many passages but could get no peace, and finally retired for my sleep. Each morning since that time, I have listened to you, but none of the messages seemed to clear up my soul, nor did they show me how to find Christ.

"Your message yesterday morning, however, was exactly suited to my need. When you quoted your text: 'Enter into thy closet and pray,' I saw the mistake I had made and the hindrance. I had been thinking that it was necessary for me to make some show of my decision. I knew of no church to which I could go and make such a confession, for I belonged to none. I had been wondering also what the other fellows on the force would think of me if I became a Christian and confessed it to them.

"As these thoughts surged through my heart, I heard you say: 'My friend with a heavy heart, if you are listening this morning, will you not just slip away alone with your Lord, and kneeling before Him, accept Him, and make Him the Lord of your life and the Savior of your soul? Believe in His finished work on Calvary for you and trust the efficacy of His precious blood.'

"I arose at once and went into a large clothes-closet, where I knelt before the Lord and told Christ that I did believe in Him, and would just then accept Him for myself. I am sure that He took me, for He gave me the peace that my heart so long desired. I am so glad that He was willing to save me after so many years of indifference to His call. I am so glad that we had the mix-up about the hats, because by this peculiar situation I was led to listen more closely and get to know you more intimately. I am sure that this broke down a little bit of opposition that was in my heart towards you and made it easier for me to believe the Bible."

Officer Clark is now in southern Kansas living for God, loving his Bible, and seeking to serve his Lord. We hope and pray that every police officer who reads this story will have a somewhat similar experience. Christ Jesus will save each one who seeks Him. Have you knelt at His cross and accepted Him for yourself? He will receive you and will not cast you out.

Jack Was Saved but Died

Outdoor shows are divided roughly into circuses, tent dramatic shows, carnivals and rides. Many excellent people are found in these various enterprises—men and women who would be saved if someone cared for their souls. Usually, Christians do not attempt to reach these people with the Gospel. Because of the worldly character of the amusement business, Christians give both it and them a wide berth. Very few really care for the souls of show-folk.

Jack was in the show business. He owned four dramatic shows, traveling through the states of the middle west. He was known as a "clean" showman. He did not use tobacco, nor did he ever swear or take the name of the Lord in vain. He had a reputation of being unusually kind to His employees and absolutely honest with the patrons who attended his shows. No lewd performance was permitted by him, nor suggestive jokes. Jack took special pride in the high caliber of his actors and the attractive plays which he produced.

One day Jack found it necessary to come to my office on business. A friendship began that day which lasted until Jack died. After transacting our business affairs, I talked with him about the Lord Jesus. He was quick to tell me how clean his business was and how good his own life was. I congratulated him on this, but assured him that it would not save his soul, nor put away a single sin.

"Jack," I said, "although you do not have as many sins as others, you have some, and those you have will shut you out of Heaven and will send you to the lake of fire. I like your honesty; I believe you have a true heart. Do let me tell you that the Lord Jesus came to save you and to make you a true Christian. Only Christ can give you eternal life. Only He can blot out your sins. He alone can bring you to God in peace."

I gave Jack some Gospel tracts to read and he promised to return. Our business together made it necessary for him to return rather often for a while.

After several visits together, and these were two or three weeks apart, Jack entered the office one day to tell me that he was leaving the city. "I have four shows out," he said, "and they are scattered around in four states. I find it necessary to visit each one of them and check them up. I probably will not get back for two or three months, for I shall stay a while on each show and see how they are being handled."

I had bought a little New Testament to give to my friend. It was beautifully bound. Some of the principal Gospel verses I had marked with a lead pencil, and had slipped bits of paper in between the leaves, so that Jack could easily find these particular portions. Handing it to my friend, I said, "Jack, I want to present to you this lovely little Testament. You will find in its pages the story I have been telling you during our visits. Before you go I would like to read with you John 3:16."

Opening to the passage, I read it slowly and distinctly — "For God so loved the world, that he gave his only begotten Son, that whosoever believeth in him should not perish, but have everlasting life." Jack listened with respectful attention. Taking him by the hand, I said, "Jack, Christ Jesus wants you. He is today sitting at God's right hand waiting to save you, to forgive you, and to make you a true child of God. Will you accept Him today before you leave?"

He pressed my hand firmly, and said "I will take Him, doctor; I need Him. I know there are sins in my life, and I know that I am not a Christian."

"Thank you, Jack." I said. "There is joy in Heaven over your decision and I know you have received a welcome, for He said, 'All that the Father giveth me shall come to me; and him that cometh to me I will in no wise cast out (John 6:37).'"

After a few more quotations, I bade my friend good-bye, and said, "I do not know, Jack, that you will ever return. Life is full of accidents, as you know; but I shall have the joy of knowing that you have trusted the Savior and that we shall be together throughout eternity. Good-bye."

A week or ten days had passed, when a letter was received from a minister in Louisiana. The news it contained was a shock to my heart. The story was that Jack was riding along on the train in a Pullman berth. A flood had loosened the supports under the trestle, so that when the train struck it the trestle gave away, and the cars were piled up in the river and on the bank. The car in which Jack was sleeping was crushed in such a way that Jack's legs were pinned in between the slashed woodwork and he could not move. The car caught fire at the opposite end from the one in which Jack was held fast. The loud noise of the accident aroused the people in the village nearby, and among those who rushed to the scene to give aid and relief was this minister. He hurried along among the cars of the wreckage, when his attention was attracted by the cries of a man caught in the burning car. He hurried to the window, broke the glass and saw my friend pinned in the bed helpless. Jack was lying there with my little Testament in his hand reading John 3:16. He had gone to sleep with it during the night and still had it when he was aroused by the wreck. The pastor saw that there was no way to deliver him and at once asked him if he knew the Lord.

"Yes," he said, "Christ Jesus saved me ten days ago in the office of my friend in Kansas City. Here is the Testament he gave me. I shall soon be burned to death by this fire. I want you to take the Testament and send word to my friend that Jack died trusting in Jesus Christ. You may keep the Testament for your trouble, but be sure to send word to the doctor. He will be glad to know."

Jack did die that morning. Frantic efforts were made to save him, but the fire spread too rapidly, and he was caught too firmly beneath the wreck. Jack died but he was saved, saved just in time. Friend, will you be caught unprepared and die lost? Or, will you accept Jesus Christ as your Lord and Savior just now and die saved?

A Giant Learned What Love Is

A very tall young man worked in the shops in the city of P——. He was a giant. He stood head and shoulders above all his fellows, was splendidly formed, and had a handsome appearance. His friends loved him. He was kind and gentle in his actions and life, but he was an unbeliever. He seemed to take great delight in finding fault with God. Those who knew him best and loved him most were Christian friends. His attitude toward the Lord was a burden on their hearts. Often they prayed for his conversion.

Mr. H——, our young giant friend, rarely entered the doors of a church. He had no interest in religion, except to make it the butt of his jokes. He was a well-educated boy and had learned many clever arguments against Christianity and in favor of his atheism.

It happened to be my lot, through the kindness of the Lord, to spend a Sunday in this city of P——, and was requested to give a message Sunday evening in the church where the friends of the giant attended. Word was sent to Mr. H—— that a physician would give a message on "The Love of God," and he was requested to attend. To the great surprise of those who asked him, he readily consented, feeling that he would rather listen to a doctor than to a preacher.

The presence of this friend and his attitude of mind were unknown to me at the time, but the Holy Spirit knew and led

me to select for my text I John 4:16 — "God is love." The subject
interested Mr. H—— very much, for he had often said that if
God is love then there could be no hell, nor will a God of love
ever punish sinful men. He could not reconcile the love of God
with the judgments of God and therefore rejected both.

The subject was developed along a threefold line: God's
love for His Son, His love for the Christians, and His love for
the lost world. I sought to show that if God loved His Son, then
He must punish the enemies of His Son; and the punishment
that God would give the enemies of Christ would prove
conclusively the love of God for His Son. I used an incident that
occurred in another city to illustrate the point.

A prominent business man in that city had turned his back
on the faith of his fathers and embraced the atheistic position
that a loving God will not punish sinners. Hearing of this
decision, I went to the office of my friend and said to him, "J—
—, you have a little daughter, have you not?"

"Yes," he said, "and I love her dearly."

"How old is she now?" I inquired.

"Just twelve," he answered.

"Do you love her, J——?"

"Do I?" he said. "I live for her. My life is planned for her
enjoyment."

"Well, J——," I said, "suppose when you go home tonight
you find a brute of a man with your little girl among the trees
surrounding your home. He is beating her, attacking her,
crushing her very life out. Suppose I am watching you to see
what you will do. How can you best prove to me that you love
your little daughter?"

I saw J——'s face redden; his lips tightened; his teeth were
grinding together; his fists were clenched; rage was in his eyes.

"Walter," he said, "that man wouldn't need an undertaker
when I got through with him. I would tear him to pieces."

I could see his deep emotion; my point had been gained.

"Jim——," I said, looking him right in the eye, "what makes
you think that the God who loves His own Son will not punish
terribly those who hate His Son and speak evil of Him?"

"Thank you, Walter," he said, "I see how foolish I have
been. I will burn that literature tonight in my furnace and
return to the faith of my mother."

As I told the story in the pulpit at P——, the giant leaned forward, gazing intently and listening with all his powers. It was a new thought to him that justice and judgment proved love. I continued with the sermon and asked, "How can God better show His love for the Christians than by separating them forever from those who hate them, and by judging and punishing those who have persecuted and injured the people of God? God will separate them as the sheep from the goats, as the tares from the wheat, as the leaven from the meal, as the false from the true. He will certainly punish the enemies of His dear people.

"God has said that He loves the world. He will prove that love by giving them what they want. Their desire is to shut out God. They want the blessings of God but not the person of God. They want the gifts of the Lord but not the presence of the Lord. Since they want to get rid of God, He can do nothing else than to send them into the outer darkness where neither He nor His blessings can be reached. The ungodly would be wretched and miserable if they were taken to Heaven; therefore, God will send them away where there is no Heaven."

The sermon was concluded. Our giant friend made for the door and hurried home. He did not want to talk with anyone; he did not wish to visit. He slipped away to his room and there during the hours of night, he cried to God for mercy. There alone he accepted the Savior.

The following morning found Mr. H—— at the phone calling up his friends. "I believe that God is love," he said. "I know He is, and instead of sending me to hell, He sent His Son to save me. God is right and I was wrong. Oh, how good He has been to accept me, when I was His enemy, and to save my soul! I am anxious to see you and to tell you all about it."

The giant became small; his pride was humbled; his self-sufficiency was brought down. He fell at the feet of Jesus Christ and became a lowly servant in the Master's service.

Perhaps you who read this story may have the same hallucination from Satan about God's judgments. Let reason prevail in your mind. Do you not see that love defends the one loved by judgment, and that God's love is expressed in the giving of His Son and in His judgment of sin?

The Lodge Organist Saw Something

An undersized Englishman came to the United States some years ago to make his home and his fortune. He was a brilliant little fellow who had been trained in the tailoring business. Mr. P—— was a very religious man, had been quite active in the little church where he was raised just south of London, and of course sought a church connection when he came to the city of L——.

Other friends had come from the same English city and had settled in L——, so Mr. P—— felt that he would be among friends and old acquaintances in his new location. The friends who had preceded Mr. P—— to this country were real believers in our Lord Jesus Christ. They knew the experience and joy of the new birth. These friends, however, did not believe that Mr. P—— had ever passed from death unto life, nor had a personal experience with the Savior. When our friend applied for membership in the church at L—— he was rejected by the elders on the ground that they did not believe in his conversion.

This decision on the part of the church leaders rather embittered Mr. P——, and a separation came about between himself and those whom he had hoped to be associated with. Being disappointed in this endeavor, he joined a certain heathenistic lodge in the city and decided to throw his influence, talent, and time into this new line of work.

Mr. P—— was quite a talented musician. This talent was soon recognized by the lodge members and he was elected as organist for the lodge. It was his duty to play during the bestowal of the various "degrees." He did this work so well that year after year for a period of twenty-five years Mr. P—— continued to serve in this capacity.

During the services required in one of the programs, the master in charge of the initiation would say, "Take him away and crucify him." Mr. P—— had often heard those words, for many candidates went through the lodge. The words had never impressed him particularly; they were only part of the ritual with no especial meaning to his heart.

Through a peculiar combination of circumstances, I had been brought rather often into the presence and company of Mr. P——. Sometimes I had the joy of being in his home; sometimes the meeting was on the street by accident. Each time my friend would remark on the harsh treatment he had received from those whom he thought were his friends. I would then seek to help him to understand the Gospel and to really trust the Savior. None of my efforts seemed to bear fruit, for Mr. P—— was quite occupied with his own goodness, his clean life, his religious activities, and other attitudes which he was convinced would be assets in the sight of God. One day word was brought to my office that Mr. P—— was quite ill in his home and was hardly expected to live. Several of us began to pray to the Lord would reveal Himself to the heart of this earnest man. The news that came from his bedside was not encouraging, until one day my telephone rang and I recognized the voice at the other end as the voice of my friend.

"I am getting better, doctor," he said. "I have had a wonderful experience and as soon as I am able I shall come down to tell you about it. Will you be in the city for a while?"

"Yes, Mr. P——," I replied. "I am so glad that our prayers have been answered and that we shall soon have the pleasure of seeing you again. I trust it will be for the glory of God."

About fifteen days after this conversation, Mr. P—— walked into my office. He was very frail and pale, showing plainly the ravaging effects of the disease on his body. He was about sixty years of age and not at all robust. The disease had well nigh taken him away. He seated himself beside by desk, trembling with emotion and with tears in his eyes.

"Walter," he said, "you know I have held a grudge against you and against others in the church because you never would accept me as a Christian. You did right; I was not a Christian; I was just a religious sinner. I am so glad that you were honest with me. Now I am saved and I have come to tell you how it happened."

As I sat looking into the eyes of my good friend, his white hair, his emaciated form, his intense earnestness, stirred my heart and I silently praised God for His wonderful love to this aged one at the end of his life.

"Do tell me about it, Mr. P——; I shall be so glad to hear the story."

"It was this way," he said. "As I was lying on my bed, terribly sick, I seemed to be in a trance or a coma, when there appeared before me quite plainly a cross. It seemed to be on the top of a hill standing out alone and silhouetted against the sky. On that cross there seemed to be a large shapeless black mass of something. It was terrible to look at. There was no form to this black object; it just seemed to hang limp and loose there on the cross. It frightened me and I was aroused.

"I could not get that vision out of my mind, while over and over again I said to myself, 'What does it mean? What is that black mass and why is it on that cross?' It seemed that each time I would fall off into a doze I was seeing that peculiar vision. It frightened me and drove away my sleepiness. Suddenly, as I lay thinking about it, those words came to me which I had heard so often in the lodge, 'Take him away and crucify him.' And then the thought came to me, 'Why did they take Him away and crucify Him? Why did He need to die?' Wasn't it strange, Walter, that I never thought of that before? Now those words seemed to burn themselves in on my heart and I could not get rid of the question. My mind, of course, was not very active, due to my illness, and the effort sent me back into a drowsy semi-conscious condition. Again the cross and the black mass loomed up before me and wakened me."

The vision and question attached themselves to each other in the mind of Mr. P—— and he pondered over both of them together. The Holy Spirit was watching this process. The Spirit of God was the author of both the vision and the question. The Lord had His eye on Mr. P—— and was reaching out His arms to gather him into His fold.

Mr. P—— continued: "It seems strange to me that I could not figure out what that black shapeless thing was on the cross, nor could I understand why they took Jesus away and nailed Him to a cross. All at once the whole matter became clear in my mind. That shapeless mass was Jesus, covered all over with my black sins. The guilt of my life and the wickedness of my heart were all there covering Christ on the cross. They took Him away and crucified Him, so that He would put away my sins. Walter, I cannot tell you how deeply my soul rejoiced when I saw that wonderful truth. I had never seen it before. The death of Christ never appealed to me as a personal blessing for myself, but then and there, lying in my bed, I said: 'Oh, Lord Jesus, I worship you! You were dying for me. You were covered with my sins. You have blotted them all out, and I am saved.'"

Mr. P—— leaned forward over my desk, extended his hand, and with deep emotion and with sobs, said: "Walter, I am your brother now; you can really accept me as a Christian now, for Jesus has saved me and my sins are gone."

He did not live very long to tell the story, but for three years before the Lord took him home, he witnessed in the lodge, in the church, and to his many business friends. His testimony was clear and enthusiastic. God made him a blessing to many.

Friend, perhaps you, too, are in the lodge with no Savior and no forgiveness of sins. Will you not come to the Lord Jesus Christ as Mr. P—— did, and make Him your own personal Savior?

The High School Teacher Was Changed

During the course of a revival meeting in the Memorial Church, a group of friends attended regularly in a body and sat near the rear of the auditorium. It was quite evident that the message had been of such a character that it instilled a deep interest and aroused some surprise in their hearts.

The ministry followed the lines of salvation by grace alone, without human merit or personal virtue. The text chosen one night was: "For by grace are ye saved through faith; and that not of yourselves, it is the gift of God; not of works, lest any man should boast" (Ephesians 2:8-9). On another night, the text was taken from Romans 4:5 — "But to him that worketh not, but believeth on him that justified the unGodly, his faith is counted for righteousness." As the interest of these friends deepened from night to night, they were led to move forward a few rows.

At the close of the first week, a lady who seemed to be the leader of this group, approached me with the statement: "This Gospel which you preach is a new one to me. Being a Sunday school teacher in a church in another part of this city, I have been active in Christian work among young people. I am also a school teacher in the public schools of this city. Your messages from night to night have caused me considerable self-examination, and I think I am beginning to understand the reason why Christ has seemed so far away from me, and why I have experienced so little in the way of spiritual results in my church work. I fear I have never been saved at all."

The earnestness of this friend, together with her frank admission of failure, assured me that the Holy Spirit was effectively working in her heart.

"What are you depending upon for salvation, Mrs. B——?"

"I do not know that I am really depending upon anything," she answered. "I know that it is right to be religious; I strive to be good; I seek to be as useful as possible in the church; and for that reason I suppose that God will be kind and merciful to me."

"Do you find anything like that in the Bible?" I asked. "What Scriptures would lead you to think that God will forgive you if you try to be good? Where have you read in the Bible that religious activities and desires for good things are sufficient to blot out the sins that you have committed?"

She looked puzzled for a moment. That she must find her instructions in the Bible seemed an entirely new thought to her. "I will look it up," she said, "and when I return another day, I will let you know."

She did return Sunday and Monday and on through the week, but avoided giving me the opportunity of speaking with her—leaving immediately, with the others in the group, as soon as the service closed. Throughout the meetings, she paid close attention to the messages, turning up the passages in her Bible as they were quoted, and checked up the speaker continually. Not until Friday night did the burden of her heart impel her come forward for further help.

At the close of the meeting on that night, I observed Mrs. B—— coming towards the front of the auditorium and so I made an opportunity for a personal conversation with her. Stepping to one side where we might be quiet, she said rather impulsively: "I am ready now to be saved. These two weeks have caused me to examine my heart carefully, and my life as well, and I find that all I have is religion. It has been a good religion and orthodox in every way as far as I can find, but there never has been a personal meeting with Christ in my experience."

Seating ourselves, I turned to the Scriptures and read to her: "Not by works of righteousness which we have done, but according to his mercy he saved us" (Titus 3:5).

"Do you suppose that this passage is true?" I asked her.

"It must be true," she replied, "although I never knew before that such a statement was in the Bible. Even now I do not understand it. It seems to me that if I do not work for salvation I will never get it. Do you mean that I should just do nothing at all to be saved? If I quit trying to be saved, will God save me anyway?"

This statement caused me to turn to Romans 5:6, which reads: "When we were yet without strength, in due time Christ died for the ungodly."

"You will never be saved, Mrs. B———, until you acknowledge your helplessness, your weakness, and your inability to save yourself."

Her response to this statement was one that I have often heard, and one that is very commonly made by those who do not see that Christ Jesus alone is the Savior from hell and the Giver of eternal life: "But doesn't the Bible say somewhere that 'faith without works is dead'? Doesn't that mean that we should believe what the Bible says and then do all the good we can, in order that we may be saved?"

"Yes," I answered, "the Bible does make that statement in James 2:20, and two examples are given in that chapter of the kind of works referred to. Neither one of the examples, however, is the kind that you have in mind. The two incidents recorded there tell of a wonderful faith and confidence in the Word of God and the will of God. The good works that you are picking out, such as helping the poor, caring for the sick, looking after the various kinds of church work and such like, only prove that you do not believe in the salvation that is in Christ Jesus, but that you believe that salvation is by works and not by Christ at all."

"I can readily see that so far nothing I have done has produced any change in my life. I have never received eternal life, although I have often read about it in the Bible, but never understood what it meant. I pray and work but seemingly it is without result, and certainly does not bring any peace or joy to my soul. It must be that there is something wrong with my faith and that I am on the wrong track. Do explain this 'Grace' business more fully to me."

Such a cordial invitation was not to be refused and I undertook to call her attention to Christ and to His cross. The passage chosen for our consideration was I Peter 2:24, wherein we read: "What his own self bare our sins in his own body on the tree."

"Whose sins did He bare, Mrs. B——?"

"He must have borne mine," she said, "for there is no other Savior, and certainly He will never return to die again for me. How strange that I never saw that passage before. Is this truth found anywhere else?"

We then turned to I Peter 3:18, and read: "Christ also hath once suffered for sins, the just for the unjust, that he might bring us to God."

"May I ask you again, Mrs. B——, for whom was Jesus dying, and for whose sins was He suffering? Do you know?"

The thought that Jesus had died for her own personal sins was such a new experience to the heart of this friend, that she seemed staggered by the wonderful revelation. It seemed too good to be true. She read and re-read the passage several times, thought carefully of each word, and then said: "I see now what I have never seen before, that Christ Jesus came to save me, and to put away my own personal sins."

"Then will you just now tell Him that you believe Him, and accept Him as God's gift to you? He says in John 1:12—'But as many as received him, to them gave he power to become the sons of God, even to them that believe on his name.' Let us look, too, at this passage in John 3:36—'He that believeth on the Son hath everlasting life: and he that believeth not on the Son shall not see life; but the wrath of God abideth on him.'"

The work was finished in her heart, and so she said, "May I come to Christ just now and tell Him that I trust Him, and that I take Him for my very own?"

"Yes, indeed," I answered quickly, "I am sure His heart will be filled with joy as He hears you tell Him of your faith and trust."

We knelt together and with deep emotion, she said: "Lord Jesus, you have been wonderful to me. You have borne with me through the years, but in my ignorance I stayed away from you, and did not know that I could come to you as a guilty sinner. I do come now, Lord Jesus, and take you as my own Savior and Lord. I believe you have blotted out my sins with your precious blood. I love you and trust you."

The heart that had been in the dark was flooded with light. The soul once dead in sins had received eternal life. The life heretofore fruitless was now on the threshold of a life of blessing and power.

Perhaps others who read this message may be passing through a similar experience. Is there a question in your heart as to why you lack peace; why the things of God are so difficult to understand; and why so little fruit is evident in your ministry and labors? Go to the Lord Jesus Christ quickly. He is God's remedy for every need of the human soul.

The Paper Carrier Made a Discovery

A young lad who had passed the fifteenth milestone of life's journey by only a few months, sought to work his way through school by means of carrying the daily newspaper. On the particular day of this story's inception, the young fellow, after covering his route and eating his supper, proceeded to the yard and began to cut the grass with the law-mower.

The evening was perfect in its setting — the weather being warm — and was typical of those proverbial June days when the fragrance of spring permeates the air. While the lad's mother sat in the front yard sewing in the twilight, an elderly gentleman drove along the street with a horse and surrey and called to the mother, "Would you not like to attend a Gospel service tonight which is being held in a tent on Flint Street? Perhaps your son would like to go with you. I will take you there and bring you back in my buggy."

Of course, the lad was none too eager to cut the grass, and grasped at the opportunity of having a "night out" in this novel fashion. Upon learning of the boy's desire to go, the mother agreed to accompany the neighbor and both prepared for the trip, eager to hear the Gospel.

The father of this young man was a preacher of the old school. His had been a very fruitful ministry in the states of Indiana and Ohio. In his home life, he had sought to make known the Gospel to the children and always insisted that they

attend Sunday school and church services. However, none of
this ministry had been the means of reaching the heart of the
newsboy. He attended the services regularly, boasted in his
belief of the Bible form cover to cover, and loved to hear it
taught.

The life of Lewis—the subject of this story—was not
exemplary. Often he merited and received severe discipline in
his home, because of an uncontrolled temper and much
selfishness. At the church, he was quite religious, taking the
place of an outstanding Christian among the young people. His
life before the public was more or less attractive, many friends
being won by his amiable character and willingness to serve.
But in the home and in his private life, Satan seemed to rule.
Many evil habits gripped his heart and controlled his life, when
not directly in the public eye.

The lad experienced times of deep anxiety of heart, because
of the bondage which these sins frequently caused. On certain
occasions, he would pray at the bedside for such a length of
time that his brother would shake him, trying to arouse him
from a supposed sleep. He would strive to drown the memory
of his sins by reading the Bible at some length. On those days
when sin particularly annoyed him and had the victory over
him, he would take part of his savings and present them as an
extra offering to the Lord in the church fund. He had a different
price for different sins. When certain sins were committed, he
would contribute to the church an extra 15 cents. Other sins
seemed more terrible, and for them he would give 25 cents
extra to the cause of the Lord. Such was the darkness of the
lad's heart, even though raised in a preacher's family and in the
church environment.

Upon one occasion, as a punishment for much
disobedience, Lewis' mother made him polish the stove in the
sitting room. While thus seated on the floor, engaged in
polishing the base of the stove, his father, the minister, passed
through the room and remarked: "Lewis, you profess to be a
Christian; you make more of a pretense at it than any of the
other boys; but in spite of this, you seem to be the worst of them
all. I with you were a real, true Christian."

This statement pierced the boy's heart like a sword. He, too,
had earnestly desired to be a real Christian. He felt that there
was something in Christianity he did not possess, and yet he

was ignorant of the fact that a greater blessing was available than that which he had already claimed.

While in this frame of mind, the youthful paper carrier gladly accepted the invitation to accompany his mother and the neighbor to the place where he would hear something that might clear up the darkness of his heart, and thus relieve the distress of his soul. Arriving at the tent where the meetings convened, they found about two hundred people congregated to listen to the speakers—two Scotchmen, who expounded the Scriptures and explained the passages as Lewis had never heard them before. The text for the evening was Romans 4:5—"To him that worketh not, but believeth on him that justifieth the ungodly, his faith is counted for righteousness." This was a new truth to Lewis—one he had never heard before, and as the speakers unfolded the passage, it was quite apparent that the lad's heart was deeply touched.

Returning home, the mother and son reviewed the sermon together. "I do not believe that there is any verse like that in my Bible, Mother," he said. "I never heard of anyone being forgiven without his working for it. Let us get our Bibles, Mother, and see if they read like his."

Obtaining them, they found that the verse read just the same in their Bibles as it read in the one which the preacher used. Lewis then retired to his room to get the lessons for the day following, for he was a sophomore in the C—— High School.

There was not much rest for the lad that night, for the preacher had emphasized the word "not" in the text and it was impressed deeply on his heart. The Holy Spirit was working, showing the boy that all of his efforts to be good were of no avail in the salvation of his soul.

The following evening, the Christian neighbor drove by again with another invitation for them to hear the Scotch preachers, and found the mother and son quite ready to attend the service. The text that evening was taken from Ephesians 2:8-9. The messenger stressed again the word "not" as he read, clearly and distinctly: "Not of works, lest any man should boast." He explained how impossible it is for a guilty sinner to clear himself of his wickedness. He described also the foolishness of the man, who being condemned and in the cell, sought by good works and good intentions to remove his condemnation, and thus to clear the records of his sinful deeds.

Again, the lad and his mother returned home to consider with profound amazement this remarkable passage and the explanation given by the minister. More and more, Lewis saw that his religious performances had no weight with God. He well remembered that through his four or five years' experience in his religious exercises, no good had been accomplished and no light had entered his soul. Frequently, he had been tempted to throw the whole business overboard and live out-and-out for the devil. The fear of future judgment and punishment were the only restraining forces which prevented his giving himself over completely to the world and turning his back on that which gave him no peace and answered none of his heart cries and yearnings.

The following night, they again attended the meeting in the tent, to hear for the third time a message on the same subject, but taken from Titus 3:5—"Not by works of righteousness which we have done, but according to his mercy he saved us, by the washing of regeneration, and the renewing of the Holy Ghost." That word "not" again presented itself vividly to the mind of Lewis, as he listened to the fervent, earnest message of the Scotchman. It rang in his ears and sank into his soul: "Not by works of righteousness"; "Not by works of righteousness"; "Not by works of righteousness which we [I] have done." His soul was in a turmoil. Formerly, he believed that the works of righteousness done in the Sunday school and in the young people's society were meritorious, and surely would be the means of obtaining favor with God. Being active in the church, he was frequently asked to put on a "clown" act in some show for the church, or to solicit money for the church debt.

The three Scriptures used in the three messages which he had heard, convinced Lewis that all of his religious activities left him as a lost sinner, without God and without hope. As the fourth night rolled around, Lewis was again found at the tent listening intently to a message from Isaiah 64:6—"All our righteousnesses are as filthy rags." That sermon completely removed every vestige of hope that remained in his heart. All of his hopes for eternity were based on his religious and righteous acts. If his works of righteousness were as filthy rags in God's sight, what must his sins be like? If the best that he had done was only an abomination to God, what must the Lord think of his sins? These thoughts occupied his mind and soul. He was at his wits end. He saw that what he possessed was rejected by the Lord, but he did not yet see that all he needed could be found in Christ.

The special meetings came to an end and Lewis was not yet saved. He disputed in his mind with the truth that he had learned and stubbornly refused to acknowledge that he was as bad as the preacher indicated. He would not take the place of being utterly lost, but rather thought there might be some development in his character which would enable him to be worthy of Heaven. Thus the summer passed, but the impressions received at the tent remained.

Another meeting was announced for December, and Lewis planned to attend. The first service was held on Sunday night. The messenger's text was John 3:16. For the first time, it became clear to the young man that Christ Jesus is the Savior; He must do all of the saving. We cannot help Him nor add to the value of either His person or His work by our religious activities. The message made a deep impression on the heart of Lewis, and he left the building determined to have the matter settled that night.

During the four-mile walk home after the meeting, our young friend found plenty of time for meditation. Having reached the corner where two main highways met, he found a bench, seated himself, and pondered over the decision which he knew he must make. Would he take Christ and receive eternal life, or would he go on with the world, in his sins, and still rely upon a smattering of religion to sweeten the path? As he thus meditated over the possibilities, the Holy Spirit brought to his mind Colossians 2:14 — "Blotting out the handwriting of ordinances that was against us, which was contrary to us, and took it out of the way, nailing it to his cross."

For the first time, the truth that Christ Jesus had borne his sins on Calvary was revealed to the heart of this seeking sinner. The blessed, watchful Spirit also brought to his mind the verse of a hymn, which Lewis repeated aloud to himself:

Payment God will not twice demand,
First at my bleeding Surety's hand,
And then again at mine.

Rising to his feet, Lewis turned his gaze to the starry heavens, saying: "Lord Jesus, I will take you, I believe you did bear my sins on Calvary, and that you blotted them out. I thank you that my sins are gone and that you are my own Savior." The burden rolled away, and Lewis now belonged to the Lord Jesus Christ. With a light heart and a buoyant step, the homeward journey was resumed.

May the telling of this story encourage many another young man to come to the Lord Jesus Christ for salvation. As you trust in the Savior who is at the right hand of God, He will be the Lord of your life and the Redeemer of your soul.

Weir Seir of the Prison

In the center of the old gray prison-yard, stands a brick building which has been converted into a chapel. It will seat about eight hundred men, and is often filled when men of God from time to time bring to these inmates the message of salvation.

One Sunday afternoon, on a dark and dreary day as the rain was falling, the men congregated in the auditorium to hear a message from the Word of God. The black prisoners sat on one side of the center aisle and near the front. There were perhaps two hundred of these, the white prisoners filling up the remainder of the room.

In one corner, near the platform, a choir arose to sing, as each hymn was announced. In the choir there were groups from both races. Some were old and some young, but all dressed alike in prison garb. A group of Christians assembled themselves on the platform, prepared to render the service of prayer or song, or the ministry of the Word, as the leader might request.

As the meeting progressed and the time came for the sermon, I announced that the subject for the hour would be found in Matthew 11:28—"Come unto me, all ye that labor and are heavy laden, and I will give you rest." One of the prisoners in the black section, I observed, was paying very close attention. He heeded not those at his side, who at times were joking and calling attention to the peculiarities of other prisoners; but his attention was riveted altogether upon the minister and his message.

The earlier part of the sermon was devoted to the preceding verse, in which the Lord Jesus said, "All things are delivered unto me." I called attention to the fact that what they had tried to obtain in paths of sin, they could receive as a gift from Christ Jesus the Lord. They were reminded that because the heart is hungry for many things, God gave Christ to supply that hunger and to satisfy every craving of the heart.

Frequently during this part of the message, Weir was seen to hang his head, as though agreeing with the fact, and remembering with sorrow his path of sin. He had found that the "way of the transgressor is hard." His life had not been an easy one, having been cast upon his own resources for some years. Although he seemed to be not over thirty-five years of age, yet in those few years he had seen much of sorrow and sin.

Far distant, in western Kansas, Weir had been arrested upon a rather serious charge, and being without friends or money, was soon sentenced to serve a term in the state penitentiary. Having been an inmate in the prison for three years at the time of this incident, he would soon be eligible for parole, although he realized that when he was paroled he would be expelled from the country as an alien. In his young manhood, he had stolen away from Liberia, NW. Africa, and made his way on a tramp steamer to the great United States, because he had heard that gold lay in the streets and wealth was the portion of all who came. Such was his hallucination and his subsequent disappointment, that for a livelihood he resorted to the business of robbing by day and by night, which of course led to his final apprehension.

As the sermon continued and verse twenty-eight was explained in detail, Weir realized that Christ was calling him to Himself. It was not religion he needed, but Christ, who alone could satisfy his restless, sinful heart. The "all" was stressed, and he realized that it included him. "Come unto me, all ye that labor and are heavy laden," appealed to his heart as a personal invitation for him to come to Christ with his sins and his sorrows. He had been seeking peace for many years, being heavy laden with guilt and sorrow of a life of disobedience; wanting rest and surely needing rest.

When the invitation was given, Weir did not immediately respond. He remained seated, unable even to indicate that he would like to come to the Savior and trust in the efficacy of His precious blood. Others professed to make Christ their own, but we were disappointed in Weir, for he did not come and would not accept the Savior. Ours was a feeling of grief and disappointment over his failure to respond, for he seemed to be the most interested one in the congregation; and to all outward appearance, he listened with intelligence and seemingly understood the message as it was presented.

At the close of the address, the guards dismissed the prisoners, and immediately they formed in line to return to the cell houses. In one of these lines stood Weir Seir with bowed head. He passed out with the crowd, and we returned to the city to pray that the Holy Spirit would finish in that heart the good work which He had begun. After a few days, I found it necessary to go to the Pacific Coast and left word in my office that personal mail be forwarded. Two days following my arrival at my destination, I received a letter from Weir in which he related the wonderful story of his meeting with the Lord in his cell.

As soon as he left the chapel that Sunday afternoon, he had gone to his cell, took his Testament and found Matthew 11:27-28, which he read while kneeling beside his bunk. His burdened heart yearned for that Savior, and his guilty soul wanted to hear the Judge say, "Son, thy sins be forgiven thee." He said to Christ: "You told me to come, and I am coming right now. You said you would give me rest, and I have come for it. I believe you do have everything I need, and that you will pardon and forgive me right now. Here I am, Lord; I accept you and I give myself to you." What peace and joy filled his heart, only his own lips could tell! The burden rolled away and was lost at the foot of the Cross.

Shortly after this happy meeting with the Lord, the warden sent word to Weir that he was eligible for parole if he wished to apply for such, having served the required time. So great was the change in Weir's life, that it was quite noticeable to the other prisoners, who began to call him nicknames, such as "The Parson," "The Preacher," "The Good Man," etc. Not only were scoffers attracted to him, but others with hungry hearts and darkened minds sought him out to find the way of salvation.

When word reached him that he might apply for parole, he asked for and received permission to see the warden personally. There in the warden's office, he related the story of his conversion and requested permission to remain the full length of his term, in order that he might be of the greatest possible help to those with whom he was associated.

The warden granted Weir's strange request, and during the remainder of his term, the Lord blessed his testimony to many hearts. When he was finally discharged from the prison, having completed his full time, a government officer met him at the gate of the prison and informed him that he was to be deported as an undesirable alien. Weir had never been naturalized; therefore the government sent him back to Liberia,—a procedure which is consistently followed with aliens who receive prison terms.

Weir rejoiced in this procedure, and wrote me a wonderful letter of thanksgiving to God for the privilege of returning to his native land with his fare all paid, a new suit of clothes, and with some money in his pocket which had been given him by the government authorities. In Liberia today, Weir Seir is preaching Christ, teaching the Bible, and winning souls for his Lord and Savior. In one of his messages, he said: "How I thank God that He permitted me to be put in prison. While I roamed around the United States, no one cared for my soul; no one spoke to me of Christ. In the prison, however, the Lord sent His servant with the message of salvation, and I heard of Jesus Christ who loved me in spite of my sins, and saved me both from the penalty and the power of my wickedness."

Let me urge every friend to read carefully Matthew 11:27-28, and see if you, too, may not find there the rest and the peace which Christ so freely gives.

Not Unless You Take It

In the little village of Berwick, the folk were greatly stirred by the ministry given in the little frame schoolhouse. Night after night, the building was crowded to capacity with earnest men and women, mostly farmers, who rejoiced in hearing the story of God's redeeming grace. Among those who came were two families, who occupied front seats near the platform each night. During the early sessions, they manifested a deep desire to know more of the truth and to find the Savior.

The congregation consisted largely of people who had not had the privilege of a college education, although they were not ignorant. They were earnest in their beliefs and energetic in their labors. They were not led to come to the service for foolish reasons, but were earnestly desiring help and blessing. No spirit of levity seemed evident during the services; still there existed a bright, happy spirit of confidence in God and of expectation, as we waited on Him for His blessing.

Charlie and Herman, accompanied by their wives night after night, came early to occupy their places and anxiously awaited the message. Although they listened intently as the speaker sought to stress the Gospel in its simplicity, yet no blessing seemed to come to their hearts. Seemingly, they agreed with all that was said, but this belief did not impart to them the peace and the joy for which their hearts hungered. The preacher introduced many Scriptures and used simple illustrations in seeking to explain the Gospel to them, and not a few angles of the Gospel were presented in the hope and prayer that these four friends would see the virtue of the Savior's person and work, and that they might be saved.

The speaker's heart was heavy, being burdened for these four friends who seemed to be seeking, and yet could not find. He reminded the Lord of His Word—"Those that seek me early shall find me" (Proverbs 8:17). Here were 'seekers' according to the first part of the verse, but they should be 'finders' according to the second part of the verse. Certainly if these friends had an honest desire in their hearts to know the Lord and to be saved by Him, they would find a ready response on the part of the Lord who came "to seek and to save that which was lost" (Luke 19:10).

One particular portion of Scripture which the Holy Spirit brought to the heart of the minister was John 1:12. This promise has been much used of the Lord in delivering souls from darkness and bringing them into personal contact with the living Christ. The passage reads: "But as many as received him, to them gave he power to become the sons of God, even to them that believe on his name." Our seeking friends who came early to the service, listened closely to every word of the text as it was read aloud, slowly and distinctly. Emphasizing the two words "received him," the speaker endeavored to show that many in the schoolroom that night believed in George Washington, but had never received him. Others believed in Kaiser Wilhelm, but had not received him. Still others there were who believed in that great President, Theodore Roosevelt, and yet had not received him. There are many, he explained, who believe about Christ, believe that He lived and died, believe that He is God's Son, and yet have not "RECEIVED HIM" for themselves.

A difficulty presented itself because of the spiritual blindness with which the hearers seemed engulfed, for neither the illustrations nor the explanations seemed to meet the need of those darkened hearts. Apparently there was deep desire to know the divine truth, but their inability to grasp it was distressing to the heart of the one who sought to unfold the precious Gospel and to reveal the living Christ to their hearts. The speaker was led to pray earnestly that the Holy Spirit might speak through his lips the life-giving Word. Referring to John 3:16, he explained that this gift which God had given, the gift of

His only begotten Son, must be definitely accepted by each
individual person, ere Christ would become his own personal
Savior. He read also Matthew 11:28, and sought to show that
the burdened heart may and must come to the person of the
Lord Jesus Christ; there he will find a welcome, and salvation
for his soul. In explaining John 7:37, he again called attention to
the invitation extended by Christ for thirsty hearts to come to
Him and find the satisfaction they sought.

Near the platform on the right side, stood a bookcase upon
which there had been placed a vase for flowers. Being empty it
was easy to pick it up and use it as an illustration. The preacher
took the vase in his hand and addressing the audience, said:
"Let us suppose for a moment that some of your friends in the
room tonight have a very bad cough. You have sent for me, as
a physician, to come to you and to prescribe for you the
necessary remedy. Allowing this vase to represent the bottle in
which I will place the medicine, I will compound the
prescription carefully, using only drugs that are fresh and
potent. The combination will be of such a character as to loosen
the mucus in the lungs, relieve the nervous paroxysms and
support the heart. Assuming you friends will agree that the
physician is dependable and trustworthy, and that the
medicine offered is the proper remedy for the trouble, I will
now place it on the table here before me and see what the effect
will be upon those who have the cough. Do you think that the
medicine will stop the cough and help the patient?"

The speaker hesitated a moment, observing the effect of the
illustration upon the audience. Suddenly the stillness of the
room was broken, as a small boy in the rear of the room arose
and spoke out suddenly and loudly, "NOT UNLESS YOU
TAKE IT." His intense earnestness stirred the audience to
alertness and the peculiar fitness of the answer was quite
obvious.

The preacher's attention was directed to the four friends on
the front seat. They seemed quite moved and for a moment a
deep perplexity seemed to possess them, only to disappear in
another moment, allowing the light of the Lord to envelop their
faces. They agreed that the medicine would do no good while
it remained in the bottle, and they realized that one could not
take it for another, but that each one must take it for himself.
Needing no further help from the pastor, each one of the four

promptly accepted Jesus Christ, and joy and peace filled their hearts. The answer of the boy, together with the illustration, were used of the Holy Spirit to reveal Christ to their hearts.

The close of the meeting brought a time of great rejoicing. These two friends with their wives had also witnessed others of their relatives and friends put their trust in the Savior, since many prayers had gone up to God that they, too, might be saved. Now the answer of peace had come. They had taken Christ and Christ had taken them.

This rich blessing will be yours, too, my friend, if you by faith will receive Jesus Christ for yourself, and let Him be the Lord of your life and the Savior of your soul.